CONTROVERSY!

Lila Perl

Marshall Cavendish
Benchmark
New York

With thanks to Noam Schimmel, Ph.D., London School of Economics and Political Science, for his expert review of this manuscript.

Other Marshall Cavendish Offices:
Marshall Cavendish International (Asia) Private Limited, 1 New Industrial Road, Singapore 536196 • Marshall Cavendish International (Thailand) Co Ltd. 253 Asoke, 12th Flr, Sukhumvit 21 Road, Klongtoey Nua, Wattana, Bangkok 10110, Thailand • Marshall Cavendish (Malaysia) Sdn Bhd, Times Subang, Lot 46, Subang Hi-Tech Industrial Park, Batu Tiga, 40000 Shah Alam, Selangor Darul Ehsan, Malaysia

Marshall Cavendish is a trademark of Times Publishing Limited
All websites were available and accurate when this book was sent to press.

Library of Congress Cataloging-in-Publication Data
Perl, Lila. • Genocide : stand by or intervene? / Lila Perl. — 1st ed.
p. cm. —(Controversy!) • Includes bibliographical references and index.
ISBN 978-0-7614-4900-3
1. Genocide—History—Juvenile literature. 2. Genocide—Religious aspects—Juvenile literature.
I. Title. • HV6322.7.P47 2011 • 364.15'1—dc22 • 2009033407

Publisher: Michelle Bisson • Art Director: Anahid Hamparian
Series Designer: Alicia Mikles • Photo research by Lindsay Aveilhe

Cover: *Descent to Genocide*, stained glass window by Ardyn Halter © 2004, Gisozi Genocide Memorial Centre, Gisozi, Rwanda.

The photographs in this book are used by permission and through the courtesy of:
Descent To Genocide Stained Glass Window by Ardyn Halter © 2004 The National Genocide Memorial, Gisozi, Rwanda: cover; David Sanger Photography/Alamy: 4; The Granger Collection, New York: 14; AFP/Getty Images: 20; Time & Life Pictures/Getty Images: 22; Popperfoto/Getty Images: 33; Getty Images: 38; AFP/Getty Images: 41; Christine Spengler/Sygma/Corbis: 43; AP Photo/Richard Vogel: 49; Alexander Joe/AFP/Getty Images: 56; Christopher Morris/Corbis: 60; Jean Marc Boujou/AP Photo: 60; Everett Collection: 63; Jose Cendon/AFP/Getty Images: 70; IPC Magazines/Picture Post/Getty Images: 72; Mike Persson/AFP/Getty Images: 78; AFP Photo EPA/ Fehim Demir: 85; Getty Images: 88; Scott Nelson/Getty Images: 92; Kerim Okten/EPA/Corbis: 97; Tang Chhin Sothy/AFP/Getty Images: 104; Finbarr O'Reilly/Reuters/Corbis: 108.

Printed in Malaysia (T)
1 3 5 6 4 2

Contents

Introduction

HOW DOES THE MASS SLAUGHTER OF INNOCENT civilians—the members of a group targeted for extinction—begin? In Nazi Germany, site of the best-known example of a systematically planned killing of a targeted group, it sometimes began with a sharp rap at the door. This alarming noise was followed by the appearance of booted and uniformed officers armed with pistols. "We are the Gestapo. Come with us." That was the way many of the Jews of Nazi Germany would remember the earliest government-sanctioned attacks against them.

At first there were individual arrests. Jewish men who were law-abiding citizens were taken from their homes and families and were sent to prisons and work camps. These arrests made by Nazi security squads were soon followed by mass arrests that included women and children, the very old, and the sick.

The Germans were both deliberate and systematic in their annihilation of those who were to be destroyed because of their ethnic heritage and their religion. They set up concentration camps and extermination camps so that if death did not come about soon enough for the doomed prisoners, often forced to perform slave labor, it could be speeded up by means of gas chambers. Their bodies could then be burned in ovens designed to do this efficiently.

This sculpture by George Segal, depicting the world turning its back to the genocide of the Holocaust, is on display at the Holocaust Memorial in San Francisco.

As a result, in a little more than six years—between 1938 and 1945—6 million Jews from all over Europe (plus 5 million other civilian "undesirables," among them Gypsies, Communists, homosexuals, and the disabled) were destroyed in what came to be widely known by the 1970s as the Holocaust. The word "holocaust," which comes from the Greek, means "wholly burnt" or "destroyed by fire."

A Polish Jew named Raphael Lemkin, who escaped the Nazi killing machine, sought a word for the crime against humanity that had been committed. In 1943 Lemkin introduced it to the world's lexicon. Henceforth all dictionaries would include the term "genocide." It is derived from *genos* (Greek for "race"; "kind") and *cide* (from the Latin *caedere*, "to kill").

Genocide differs from civil and political wars, in which great numbers of both combatants and civilians die, in that genocide has a particular intention. Its aim is the deliberate destruction of a racial, tribal, ethnic, national, or religious group, generally within a sovereign nation but also outside its borders, as in Nazi-occupied Europe.

Such cultural mass murders have been going on since the earliest times. The Old Testament reports (in Deuteronomy 25: 17–19) that God commanded the Israelites to "blot out" the tribe of the Amalekites from their land. And recorded history tells us of religious genocides, such as the anti-Muslim and anti-Jewish Crusades and the Spanish Inquisition of the Middle Ages. The discovery of the New World led to new instances of ethnic and racial genocide directed at the American Indian population and at the greatly expanded population of African slaves on American soil.

The twentieth century, despite its periodic claims to the attainment of global peace and human enlightenment, produced horrifying genocidal struggles and the greatest number of resulting deaths in history. These genocides include Turkey's campaign (1915–1918) to expel and destroy its Armenian population (1.5 million deaths); Germany's extermination (1938–1945) of Europe's Jews (6 million deaths); Cambodia's Khmer Rouge regime's (1975–1979) fight against classism (2 million deaths); Serbia's campaign (1992–1995) to destroy Bosnia's Muslims (100,000 deaths); and Rwanda's (1994) Hutu against Tutsi tribal conflict (800,000 deaths).

The opening years of the twenty-first century witnessed yet another genocidal operation that has so far killed some 400,000 men, women, and children who were living mainly as subsistence farmers and herders in a harsh, semiarid region of Africa. So far, it has driven 2.5 million people from their homes. This genocide is taking place in the western portion of the nation of Sudan, in a region known as Darfur, "Land of the Fur." The Fur people, along with the Masalit and the Zaghawa, are the region's major inhabitants—a total of 6 to 7 million people.

The genocide in remote and drought-ridden Darfur became known to the rest of the world in 2003. The government of Sudan had targeted a segment of its population for extermination and had assigned deputies to carry out the task. The assailants were not helmeted storm troopers, as they were in Germany in 1938. They were warriors mounted on horses or camels. Many wore Bedouin garb, long white sheaths and headdresses of cloth wrapped tightly against the sand, wind, and sun.

Armed with guns and brazenly twirling their weapons in the air, these riders are known as "devils on horseback." Their name, Janjaweed, is believed by some to be derived from the Arabic *jinn*, meaning "spirit," and *jawad*, meaning "horse"—thus "evil horsemen." Or, the name may simply mean warrior.

The Janjaweed, supported by Sudan's president and his administration, have been attacking the small villages of Darfur. These villages are often home to only a few hundred people, who are mainly of African (rather than Arab) descent. The Arab militiamen have most often made their attacks in the early-morning hours. In some cases the horsemen are preceded by government transport planes or by combat helicopters, which drop improvised bombs. The object of sending the aircraft is to create panic and disarray, making it easier for the Janjaweed to accomplish their goals of causing destruction and death on the ground. They burn villagers' houses, loot their belongings, steal their cattle, mutilate and murder the men, rape the women and girls, and leave helpless babies to die. Homeless, the surviving villagers may end up in an internally displaced persons (IDP) camp or wander across the border to a refugee camp in the neighboring country of Chad.

Although the government of Sudan (GOS) has repeatedly denied involvement in the activities of the Janjaweed, there has been extensive evidence since the first blows were struck that it is supporting the militia. Some members of this ragtag force, ranging from discharged soldiers, to the unemployed, to Arab youth gangs, fanatics, and bandits, are paid a salary by the GOS and are supplied with uniforms and weapons.

Why is this brutal assault taking place?

Sudan, geographically the largest country in Africa, appears to be in a race war against its African inhabitants. The Islamic government of President Omar Hassan al-Bashir, headquartered in the country's capital, Khartoum, is not at odds with the religion of the Darfuris, as most of them are Muslims. But it does discriminate against their black African rather than Arabic "racial" origin.

To the Arab elite, who live mainly in the rich riverine region of Sudan, where the Blue Nile and the White Nile meet, there is a history of disdain for the *zurug* ("darkness of skin color") of others in their country. In short, Arab Muslims condemn African Muslims for being "too dark." This charge, however, has little basis in fact. Arabs and Africans have intermingled in Sudan for centuries, and the groups have in many cases become indistinguishable.

As a result of the long-standing racial prejudice of the central government toward the Darfuri, their homeland experienced years of neglect and marginalization. Darfur's inhabitants were taxed but were denied basic services, such as roads, schools, health care, and the chance for economic development. The GOS also failed to respond to the region's recurring droughts and resulting famines, despite the nation's having experienced increased prosperity due to its oil wealth, making it a favored trading partner of China.

In 2002 the GOS was involved in peace talks concerning its long civil war with its black-African Christian and animist (or nature- and spirit-worshiping) subjects in the south of the country. At the same time, an insurgency flared up in Darfur.

Two rebel Darfuri groups sprang into action. In early 2003 the first—the Sudan Liberation Army (SLA)—carried out a series of attacks on Sudanese army posts and garrisons in Darfur and targeted the country's El Fasher airport. The operation killed thirty government soldiers and two officers and blew up two transport bombers and three combat helicopters of the type already being used to "soften up" the villages of Darfur for the murderous raids of the Janjaweed.

The three hundred or so guerrillas of the early SLA were made up in part of former Darfuri police and self-defense groups, who had been fighting the marauding Sudanese Arabs since the late 1990s. Others were students and intellectuals drawn to the cause for cultural as well as military reasons. Among the SLA's goals was the separation of religion and government.

The second of the insurgent organizations was the Justice and Equality Movement (JEM). It was an idealistic organization that sought equal rights, basic services, and social justice for all Sudanese under the banner of a benevolent Islamic state.

In response to ongoing rebel attacks, mainly by the SLA, that killed hundreds of the Sudanese military, the GOS encouraged more vigorous attacks on the civilian population of Darfur by the Janjaweed.

They came with horses and a lot of weapons. They are composed of Arabs from the area and others from far away. They attacked women, men and children . . . at least 240 people. This is more than half the population of [the village of] Garadai which counts 400 inhabitants. They killed mainly the young men although many old and disabled people were killed because they were not able to get out of their [burning] houses.

This eyewitness report from August 2003 is one of several published by Amnesty International. A survivor of another attack in the same month on the village of Jafal recounted the following:

The Janjaweed were accompanied by soldiers. They attacked the people saying: You are opponents to the regime, we must crush you. As you are Black, you are like slaves. Then the entire Darfur region will be in the hands of the Arabs. The government is on our side, it gives us food and ammunition.

The destruction of numerous villages throughout the region led to a mass exodus by the survivors, who had been stripped of their most basic necessities, from cooking pots to digging tools. Some sought refuge near larger towns or in makeshift desert camps, where they fashioned shelters out of domed sticks covered with plastic trash bags.

The displaced Darfuris remained in danger from the marauding Janjaweed, especially when they left their huddled encampments in search of water and firewood. Young girls and women, who were the principal gatherers of these essentials, were especially at risk from rape by the "devils on horseback." Many of the victims were children as young as seven and eight.

By early 2004 masses of refugees from burned-out villages and from displaced-persons camps in Darfur had begun to flee across the western border of Sudan into the neighboring country of Chad. Even there the Janjaweed raiders, who had no trouble crossing the dry riverbed that served as the border between the two countries, pursued them and caused further deaths. How far would the GOS and its surrogate militia go in committing its genocidal acts? Would the world take notice and, when it did, how would it respond?

Early inattention to the Darfur crisis was due partly to indifference and partly to confusion. In the view of the world's nations and international bodies, there was always an "African crisis" going on somewhere on the continent. Also, fighting had been going on between the GOS and non-Muslim African rebels in the south of Sudan for twenty years. Wasn't the situation in the west just more of the same?

Gradually it became clear that the events in Darfur were a different kind of engagement. Their aim was murder by violent means and the creation of a concentrated and helpless refugee population that could then be targeted and annihilated as well.

The first to respond to the humanitarian crisis in Sudan were aid organizations sponsored by the United Nations, by foreign governments, and by nongovernmental organizations (NGOs) that delivered food and medical supplies. But these efforts were only sporadically successful.

Although President al-Bashir promised the relief agencies free access to the refugee camps, a variety of roadblocks, both actual and invented, soon cropped up. And even when the occasional aid shipment did arrive, it immediately became the target of Janjaweed raiders, who looted the supplies and committed brutal acts as necessary.

As a result, the refugees actually became fearful of receiving relief supplies. When, early in 2004, the United States proposed mediation to aid humanitarian deliveries, Sudan's secretary of state for foreign affairs replied, "They have a right to propose and we have a right to decide. The U.S. proposal does not conform to our vision, which considers that the conflict is a matter regarding only the sons of Darfur."

The outside world was being told by the GOS to disregard all aspects of the conflict. As a sovereign state, Sudan did not welcome suggestions for alleviating the deaths of its subjects either by starvation or at the hands of the Janjaweed, even though by late 2004 the famine in Darfur, caused by the Janjaweed and the GOS, was more severe than the worst drought-induced famines of the past.

What could foreign nations and world diplomatic bodies such as the European Union (EU), the United Nations (UN), and the African Union (AU) do to stop the killing? On September 9, 2004, U.S. secretary of state Colin Powell, speaking before the Senate Foreign Relations Committee, declared that the killing of black Africans in Arab-led Sudan was "a coordinated effort, not just random violence." Therefore it must be tagged as the most condemned act in world history—it was nothing short of genocide.

What effect did Powell's censure of Sudan have? Did it mean that the United States, deeply engaged in its recent invasion of Iraq, embroiled in the ensuing war, and highly unpopular in the Muslim world, would undertake the military invasion of Sudan? Hardly.

Did other members of the community of nations, despite their widespread commitment to the UN's 1948 Geneva Convention calling for action under international law, take meaningful steps to halt the genocide? No.

The immediate results, in fact, were limited. On November 19, 2004, the UN Security Council issued Resolution 1574, voicing "serious concern at the growing intensity and violence in Darfur, the dire humanitarian situation, continued violation of human rights, and repeated breaches of the ceasefire." The resolution would prove to have no effect on the mounting death toll.

The African Union, an affiliation of African nations, which

had been monitoring the situation in Darfur with the right only to observe and report, asked the GOS for permission to increase its representative contingent from a few hundred peacekeepers to two thousand. Only a fraction of that number was accepted.

Four years later, with the death toll rising in Darfur and more than 2.5 million displaced, the genocide—having dipped in and out of the world headlines—raged on. By July 2008, ten African Union peacekeepers had been killed, and the prosecutor of the ten-year-old International Criminal Court was seeking an arrest warrant for Sudanese president Omar Hassan al-Bashir.

In the midst of ongoing violations of human rights by means of massacre, mutilation, maiming, rape, and starvation, global citizens are left with the question of how they should react. To what degree are we required to inject ourselves into the situation? Why have most genocidal powers been allowed to fulfill their deadly goals, while others have been halted by outside forces, albeit belatedly?

This question is a source of controversy both in the United States and the world over. No one can deny that genocide is the most heinous of crimes. Yet none can agree on the moral obligations of those who find themselves looking on with horror and guilt.

These men stand among the skulls and corpses of Armenian victims of genocide by the Turks.

1 Genocide Victims During the World Wars: The Armenians and the Jews

Although the word "genocide," coined in 1943, sprang from Nazi Germany's annihilation of 6 million Jews, an example of this crime against humanity had taken place earlier in the twentieth century. It was committed during World War I, between 1915 and 1918, by the Turkish rulers of the Ottoman Empire, a sprawling Muslim state in the Near East. The victims of the genocide were the Armenians, a Christian people who had lived under the Ottoman Turks since the fourteenth century.

The Armenians of Turkey and the Jews of Germany, as it turned out, had a great deal in common. Both were adherents of an ancient religion. Both were religious minorities in their respective countries. Neither had a homeland of their own and would be driven in search of a nation to house the survivors of the genocide. Both had experienced a history of persecution.

The international community had been completely aware of the intention of the respective governments of their home nations to not only destroy their culture but to murder as many of the individuals who comprised it as possible. The witnessing countries also had detailed evidence of the methods of destruction used by the genocidal powers. Yet the world had looked on, and the genocides proceeded without any action being taken to halt the killing.

Nor did the memory of the Armenian genocide restrain the enactment of Germany's Jewish genocide, only a little more than twenty years later. In late August of 1939, days before Hitler's September 1 invasion of Poland (with its population of more than 3 million Jews slated for extermination), his instructions to his killing squads were to show no mercy in their genocidal acts. "Who today, after all," Hitler queried, "speaks of the annihilation of the Armenians?"

The Jews of German-ruled Europe were ordered, as Nazi power grew and advanced across national borders, to identify themselves by wearing a Star of David drawn on yellow cloth pinned to their outer clothing. The six-pointed star, a sacred religious symbol that Hitler chose as a "badge of shame" to set the Jews apart, was only one of many such markers. Throughout the Jews' long history, anti-Semitic regimes had required the wearing of other such badges, as well as garments of various colors and design.

Similarly, the Armenians, who for centuries lived as subjects of the sultan who ruled the Ottoman Empire, had been obliged to wear certain colors and styles of clothing that would distinguish them from the Muslim majority. At one time they were forbidden to dress in silk, furs, and other valuable materials and were not allowed to wear turbans.

As *dhimmi*, who were seen as an infidel people living under Muslim sovereignty, the Armenians had limited civil and religious rights. They did have the privilege of being allowed to practice their Christian religion but were forced to pay a special tax that was not levied on Muslims. They were allowed to administer their own school systems and also to legislate matters of marriage and inheritance within their community.

In an Ottoman court, however, they had almost no legal rights.

The testimony of a dhimmi was not accepted, a Muslim who killed a dhimmi was generally not executed, and a dhimmi man could not marry a Muslim woman. In all things Armenians had to show deference to Muslims. They could not ring church bells within hearing of worshipers in a mosque, could not remain mounted on a horse if a Muslim was passing, could not build a house that was higher than that of a Muslim. All of these restrictions were the result of deep religious prejudice.

As Armenian men could hardly be trusted to defend Islam in times of war, they were exempt from military service. Yet a longtime practice of the Ottomans had been the "collection" of boys from Christian families for the purpose of converting them to Islam. Thus these youths could be put to work serving in the Ottoman military and civil service. The taking of young boys from their families was known as *devshirme.*

Another demand of the Ottoman rulers was that Armenian families house Turkish army units, often for long periods through the winters. During their quartering the soldiers received the families' best lodging space and food and often abused their privileges by committing theft and rape.

Centuries of Armenian frustration and silence reached a breaking point in the mid– to late 1800s, as progressive ideas from the West seeped into the vast Ottoman domain. Contacts with Europe, made through reading, study, and travel, acquainted members of the repressed minority with the principles of human rights and liberty. The United States contributed enlightenment as well, as American Protestant missionaries began to circulate through the Armenian communities of the Ottoman Empire.

The Armenian Apostolic Church, founded in 301 CE, had its own ceremonies and forms of worship, so its believers did not for the most part adopt the religious rituals of the American missionaries. But the visitors from afar brought other benefits to the Armenian people. As many of the missionaries were female, they advanced education for women, establishing schools, cultural centers, and colleges in key cities and provinces.

Liberal thought gave rise to Armenian activism. Secret societies as well as openly revolutionary political parties sprang up, aimed at wresting self-rule or at least a noncorrupt form of constitutional government from the Ottoman overlords.

Sultan Abdülhamid II, who had come to the throne in 1876, was less than pleased with the increasing demands of the Armenians. The European powers had already condemned him for the massacres of his non-Muslim subjects in the Balkans, where Christian Serbs and Bulgarians were clamoring for independence. The people of the Balkan lands under Ottoman rule would eventually win their independence. But the Armenians were scattered throughout Ottoman Turkey. What was the answer to the so-called Armenian Question?

The Armenian Genocide of 1915–1918

World War I, known in its time as the Great War, was chosen by the Ottoman Empire as an opportunity to recover from its status as "the sick man of Europe." Over a span of five hundred years, from the fourteenth to the nineteenth century, Ottoman fortunes had risen to a peak (in the mid–sixteenth century) and then fallen into gradual decline.

By the time the crumbling empire entered World War I in 1914, on the side of Germany and against Britain, France, and Russia, it had lost its numerous holdings in southeastern Europe, including Serbia, Bulgaria, Greece, and surrounding lands. In an effort to reestablish the empire's former wealth and glory and to expand it in an easterly direction as well, a group of reforming patriots popularly known as the Young Turks forced the sultan to concede political power to them.

The Young Turk political party was formally known as the Committee of Union and Progress (CUP). As its founders called

The Hamidian
Massacres
of the 1890s

Between 1894 and 1896 Sultan Abdülhamid II was to unleash a series of savage attacks on the Armenian people in provinces all over the country and in Constantinople, the capital (today called Istanbul). For the purpose of terrorizing, looting, and murdering the Christian minority, the sultan created a force of more than 16,000 cavalry troops known as the Hamidiye ("belonging to Hamid") regiments.

Scattered around the country in more than thirty regiments of about 500 to 1,150 men each, the Hamidiye were drawn from the Kurdish population of the Ottoman Empire. Also a minority group and often a restive and even warlike one, the Kurds were a nomadic, pastoral people who practiced their own form of Islam.

In organizing the Kurdish horsemen to spread terror throughout the Armenian settlements, the sultan was using one minority group to subdue another. Kurds who did not bow to the Turkish authorities were themselves threatened with persecution. The sultan's method was somewhat similar to that of the Sudanese president Omar Hassan al-Bashir, delegating the Janjaweed in the opening years of the twenty-first century to drive the people of Darfur from the land.

As early as 1891 the British consul to the Ottoman Empire reported from the northeastern province of Erzurum that "The measure of arming the Kurds is regarded with great anxiety here . . . the Kurds themselves . . . openly state that they have been appointed to suppress the Armenians." The Kurds also declared that they had "received assurances that they will not be called to answer before the tribunals for any acts of oppression committed against Christians."

The Hamidian massacres at the hands of Kurdish warriors on horseback erupted over Armenian protests against unreasonable and excessive taxation and over calls for reforms, such as equality with Muslims before the law. The atrocities appeared to be totally out of proportion to the demands of the Armenian activists. American missionary and relief workers reported rapes on a massive scale, the bayoneting and shooting of "men, women, and children . . . most barbarously slaughtered . . . houses fired and the inmates driven back into the flames."

In all, some 200,000 Armenians were murdered in the Hamidian massacres of 1894 to 1896. The United States, through the Red Cross and other humanitarian groups, sent aid to the survivors, who were dying of hunger and disease. The European powers strongly registered their protests through their foreign missions and their ambassadors. Yet the massacres played themselves out and would serve as the curtain-raiser to the Armenian genocide of 1915–1918.

Armenians were massacred in Constantinople, Turkey, in 1896 after Armenian revolutionaries attacked the Ottoman Bank.

themselves reformers, the Armenian population of the Ottoman Empire hoped for a time that the scaling back of the sultan's authority might improve their situation as an oppressed minority.

The Armenian communities soon learned, however, that the Young Turk movement fiercely favored an expanded Turkey that was to incorporate Turks from beyond its borders but that must also be "cleansed" of all non-Turkish peoples. The term "ethnic cleansing"—ridding the nation of nonethnic peoples—would thus be applied. In the words of Mehmet Talaat, one of the triumvirate that then controlled the government, "Turkey belongs only to the Turks."

By the spring of 1915, with the war in progress, the Turkish government launched its plans to liquidate the 2 to 3 million Armenian people who were living among the country's nearly 30 million Turks. The methods they used included roundups of able-bodied men who were either shot en masse by killing squads or marched away for deportation. The families they left behind—women and children, elderly and infirm relatives—were instructed to prepare to leave their homes, taking only a minimum of possessions. Often they were given vague promises of being allowed to return when the war was over.

Their fate, however, was to be driven forever from their villages and to lose their lives through death marches (forced by the military to plod on without food or water until they collapsed) and massacres within Turkey's borders, through being forcibly drowned by their Turkish overlords in the Black Sea, and through exile into the harshness of the neighboring Syrian Desert. More Armenians are believed to have died in Syria—of thirst, starvation, and disease—than anywhere else.

Although Christian Armenian men were prohibited from serving in the military, it had been decided at the beginning of the war that they would be useful as labor battalions. Henry Morgenthau, the U.S. ambassador to Turkey in 1915, described their duties

Mobilisation scene near Constantinople. Once t finest of fighting men, the Turks fared badly in the Balkan War. Uer German officers they rallied again in October, 1914, against the cause civilisation in Europe.

Recruits from Anatolia leaving a steamer at Cotantinople. Formerly only the Moslem Turk was liable for military serve, but the Young Turks instituted a law making every Turkish subjeciable to be called up,

Turkish Lancers leaving the Ottoman capital : their way to the front. Our photograph is eloquent of the change :uniform and equipment brought about by the German military men. But the change did not extend very far. When Turkey threw inor lot with the cause of Kaiser Wilhelm, the angements for providing the troops with clothing broke down entirely, a one result was that the men had to undertake a winter campaign inotton summer garments, and suffered terribly, especially in the Caucas. Inset : Turkish infantry on the march.

THE "SICK MAN OF EUROPE" RALLIES AT THE KAISER'S CALL.

In 1914, the Young Turks were mobilized against the Armenians.

and their treatment in his book *Ambassador Morgenthau's Story*, published at the end of the war, in 1918.

The Armenians "had been transformed into road labourers and pack animals. Army supplies of all kinds were loaded on their backs, and, stumbling under the burdens and driven by the whips and bayonets of the Turks, they were forced to drag their weary bodies into the mountains of the Caucasus."

By February 1915, however, following a humiliating defeat at the hands of the Russians, the Turkish government ordered the massacre of Armenian men in the army's labor battalions, on the grounds that they had been supportive of the Russians. The slaughter of the former army laborers was vividly described in *Ambassador Morgenthau's Story.*

> In almost all cases, the procedure was the same. Here and there squads of 50 or 100 men would be taken, bound together in groups of four, and then marched out to a secluded spot a short distance from the village. Suddenly the sound of rifle shots would fill the air, and the Turkish soldiers who had acted as the escort would sullenly return to camp.
>
> Those sent to bury the bodies would find them almost invariably stark naked, for, as usual, the Turks had stolen all their clothes. In cases that came to my attention, the murderers had added a refinement to their victims' sufferings by compelling them to dig their graves before being shot.

The annihilation of the labor battalions was only the beginning of the genocidal actions of the spring of 1915. April 8 saw the first deportation orders carried out, the residents of the affected town marched away on foot or occasionally removed by rail.

On April 24, the day before the Allied armies invaded Turkey, approximately 250 Armenian political leaders and intellectuals in Constantinople were rounded up and killed. Mass arrests in the capital followed. By May more than 2,300 of the city's most distinguished Armenian residents had been apprehended and sent to the interior to be murdered by the state.

Although the British and French enemies of the Turks protested these and other crimes taking place throughout the country, they were busy waging war against the Turks' German allies on a number of fronts in Europe. The United States was well informed about the atrocities taking place in Turkey. Its ambassador, Henry Morgenthau, cabled the U.S. State Department on July 16, 1915, with the words, "Deportation of and excesses against peaceful Armenians is increasing and from harrowing reports of eye witnesses it appears that a campaign of race extermination is in progress under a pretext of reprisal against rebellion."

On October 7, 1915, a headline in the *New York Times* read "800,000 Armenians Counted Destroyed." By the end of the year close to one million were believed to have lost their lives to the genocide, which would continue until 1918 and claim a total of 1.5 million lives. Nor did Turkey's defeat and the conclusion of World War I mean the end of Armenian oppression. Massacres and expulsions were carried out between 1920 and 1922, leading to tens of thousands more victims of the fierce campaign to render Turkey completely free of its Armenian population.

The Armenian Genocide: As the World Looked On

Although the United States did not enter World War I until 1917, no other nation was more deeply aware of the ongoing atrocities of the Armenian genocide or more closely concerned with rescue and relief efforts. America's interest was due in large part to the work of Protestant missionaries who had been active in the Ottoman Empire from the time of the Hamidian massacres of 1894–1896.

Reports by missionaries, church personnel, medical workers, educators, and general observers; by American consuls in Turkish cities; and by Ambassador Henry Morgenthau in Constantinople all revealed the extent and the cruelty of the Armenian genocide. In addition to the killings, both immediate and extended, the Turkish government used torture on designated individuals.

The bastinado, a form of punishment inflicted by beating the soles of the feet with a thin rod until they swelled and burst, was

The Turkish Killing Squads

Cleansing Turkey of its Armenian population; destroying homes, schools, and churches; appropriating Armenian property and other holdings; and blotting out all evidence of Armenian culture required the creation of a governmental body known as the Special Organization (SO). How else were the on-site exterminations, the death marches and the deportations in cattle cars, and the sinking of barges filled with Armenian refugees in the Black Sea to be carried out?

The duty of the SO was the formation of killing squads not unlike the Einsatzgruppen, or mobile killing units, that Germany was to employ twenty years later for the roundup and instant execution of Jews and other enemies of the Nazi regime.

In Turkey the killing squads were commanded by military officers but were made up of ex-convicts (many released from prisons for the purpose), outlaws and ruffians, and Kurdish tribesmen. Known as *chetes*, these killer bands were motivated by the principle of jihad, or holy war against nonbelievers in Islam, and doubtless even more so by the opportunity to pillage and rape.

Efficient killing operations by the 30,000 or so chetes could lead to the acquisition of Armenian booty and spoils, for the stripped and helpless victims were forced to leave behind their personal property and wealth. The killer bands also searched the garments of their Armenian prisoners for gold coins or other small treasures sewn into the seams or linings.

Arrests and deportation of Armenian citizens were also carried out by military police known as gendarmes, who had local and provincial jurisdiction. These officers might be compared to the Gestapo of Hitler's Germany, who conducted searches within the community for people attempting to hide themselves or their possessions from the authorities.

only one of several methods employed. Hairs were pulled from eyebrows and beards one by one, fingernails and toenails were extracted, and hands and feet were nailed to pieces of wood in a mocking reminder of the crucifixion of Christ.

Objections from Ambassador Morgenthau to the Turkish government were met with assertions that the treatment of the Armenians was purely a domestic affair. As no American lives or American interests were being affected, Turkey saw no reason for American complaints. By October 1915 relief funds from churches, the Rockefeller Foundation, the Committee on Armenian Atrocities, and other private groups began pouring into the country. But the U.S. government, despite the sinking of the British ship *Lusitania* by a German submarine in May 1915, which cost more than one hundred American lives, was still two years away from entering the war.

When finally in 1917 President Woodrow Wilson, persuaded by growing sentiment around the country for the support of international humanitarian ideals, relinquished his stance of neutrality, he declared war against only two of the enemy nations, Germany in April and Austria in December. He refused to declare war on Turkey. Like so many American heads of state who followed him, he was reluctant to expand the war effort and felt that the offer of humanitarian aid to victims of the genocide was sufficient.

Oddly enough, Wilson was also influenced by the missionary community, which had so strongly established itself in Turkey, owning property on which schools, hospitals, and orphanages had been built. The real estate holdings of the foreign mission groups were estimated to be worth $123 million. Once the United States became an enemy combatant on Turkish soil, however, these vast holdings would be subject to confiscation by the Turks. Furthermore, as the missionary groups pointed out, they would no longer be in a position to offer what aid and sanctuary they could to the Armenian widows and orphans.

When the war ended in November 1918 with an Allied victory, it was Great Britain, followed by France and Russia, that led the demand for tribunals to punish the guilty members of the Turkish leadership for crimes against humanity. The United States did not take part. It had, after all, never even declared war on Turkey.

Only a handful of death sentences by hanging were carried out. Other guilty parties received jail sentences with hard labor. Among the relatively few direct perpetrators of the genocide from whom retribution was exacted was Mehmet Talaat, or Talaat Pasha, a member of the Young Turk triumvirate. Along with many other high-ranking officials, Talaat had been given asylum in Germany, where he was living incognito.

On March 14, 1921, Talaat was shot to death on a Berlin street by a twenty-four-year-old Armenian genocide survivor, Soghomon Tehlirian. "This is to avenge the death of my family!" the young man cried as he placed the mouth of the pistol against the back of Talaat's head. In 1915 Tehlirian had been part of a deportation march on which his sisters had been raped, his brother's head had been split open with an axe, and his mother had been shot. After receiving a blow on the head that rendered him unconscious, Tehlirian awoke amidst a pile of corpses. His entire family had been murdered.

At Tehlirian's trial later that year, he was acquitted of murder on the grounds of temporary insanity and lived the rest of his life in California. He had seen his act as the culmination of a pledge for the redemption of the human conscience.

What can we say about the national conscience of the United States? Was Wilson right to keep American troops out of Turkey during World War I? In protecting the property of the missionary groups and preserving American military and political interests in the Near East, was his behavior self-serving? Did he set the pattern of foreign relations that prevails to this day, whereby the United States often overlooks a nation's internal injustices for the advantages of a profitable economic relationship?

Although the present-day Republic of Turkey continues to adamantly deny the genocide of the Armenian people during World War I, the United States maintains close relations with Turkey (a North Atlantic Treaty Organization, or NATO, member) for the purpose of keeping naval and air bases in that volatile region and promotes membership for Turkey in the European Union.

The Crime of Nazi Germany Is Named

The terrible conflict of World War I ended in 1918 with the victory of Britain, France, Russia, and the United States over Germany and its Austrian and Turkish allies, and an estimated total of 10 million military personnel dead. Ironically, the "war to end all wars," as it was popularly called in its day, laid the groundwork for World War II, which was to break out in 1939.

The peace terms dictated by the victors in 1918 were punishing. Germany was forced to disarm, give up territory, and pay reparations. A severe economic depression ensued, the government failed and, by 1933, the Austrian-born dictator-to-be Adolf Hitler rose to power.

Vowing to rearm Germany and restore its honor, the violently anti-Semitic leader of the National Socialist, or Nazi, Party crushed all political opposition and instituted laws that deprived Germany's Jews of their rights as citizens. At the same time he built a vast propaganda and law-enforcement machine, ranging from the Hitler Youth groups to the Gestapo spy agency and the murderous Einsatzgruppen, or mobile killing squads.

Hitler's assault on the Jews of Germany was more methodical and even more deadly in terms of civilians murdered than that of the Ottoman Empire on the Armenians. Starting in 1933, he ordered all Germans to boycott Jewish shops and businesses, ensuring that they would be forced to close. In 1935 he passed laws that clearly distinguished Jews from the so-called pure-blooded Aryans, characteristically fair-haired and blue-eyed ethnic Germans, or

Nordic types. Jewish children could not attend German schools; Jewish doctors, educators, and other professionals were forbidden to practice; and Jews had to have their papers stamped with an identifying J for *Jude*—Jew. Little overt opposition to Hitler's anti-Jewish policies sprang up. The emotions of the non-Jewish German population ranged from fear of retribution, should they protest, to enthusiastic support.

The violent government-implemented attacks on Jewish synagogues, schools, hospitals, orphanages, and homes on the 9th and 10th of November 1938 signaled the beginning of open warfare against the Jews who had not yet fled Germany. This event of smashing, shattering, burning, looting, and otherwise destroying Jewish property, from sacred Torah scrolls in synagogues to shop windows to pianos heaved from the balconies of private homes, was known as Kristallnacht—Night of Broken Glass.

The arrest of Jews had by that point become widespread, the victims taken without warrants or other official complaint documents to labor and concentration camps within Germany, among them Dachau and Buchenwald. The two camps were the first to have been built for the express purpose of incarcerating Jews and others seen as enemies of the regime, Dachau in 1933 and Buchenwald in 1937. There, the "disappeared" languished while anxious families besieged the offices of the Gestapo, or secret police, for news of their loved ones.

For Hitler the cleansing of Germany to make it *Judenrein*—free of Jews—was only the beginning of the "improvements" he sought to make. He was determined to take control of more of Europe than Germany had ever possessed—Austria and Czechoslovakia in 1938, Poland in 1939 (igniting World War II with Britain and France), Denmark and Norway, Belgium, Luxembourg, the Netherlands, and France in 1940.

In all of these countries, Jews, Gypsies, Communists, political and religious leaders who disagreed with the Nazi doctrine, and other nonconformists would be slated for imprisonment and eventual extermination. New concentration camps would be built, ranging from Westerbork in the Netherlands—a holding and transit camp for Jews—to the dreaded Auschwitz/Birkenau complex and other death camps in Poland. The occupied countries thus became new strongholds of Nazi oppression.

Meanwhile, the slaughter of Poland's more than 3 million Jews (the Jewish population of Germany had been only 500,000) could not proceed fast enough for the Nazi killing machine to dispose of the overflow of prisoners. Gas chambers and cremation ovens were still in the process of being built. So the Nazis sent their mobile squads, the Einsatzgruppen, into the cities and towns of both Poland and neighboring Lithuania.

In the summer of 1941 an underground Polish organization known as the Jewish Labor Bund reported, "Men, fourteen to sixty years old, were driven to a single place, a square or a cemetery, where they were slaughtered or shot by machine guns or killed by hand grenades. They had to dig their own graves. Children in orphanages, inmates in old-age homes, the sick in hospitals were shot, women were killed in the streets. In many towns, Jews were carried off to an 'unknown destination' and killed in adjacent woods."

Prior to the completion of the gas chambers in the death camps, the Nazis successfully gassed one thousand Polish Jews per day by cramming them (as many as ninety at a time) into mobile gas vans. Before the corpses were buried or burned, gold rings, gold teeth, hair, and clothing were salvaged and sent back to Germany.

Reports of the killings in Poland were received and released by Szmul Zygielbojm, a Polish Jew who made them public on the BBC in London in June 1942. As the situation worsened, Zygielbojm pleaded with American officials (the United States had entered the war in December 1941) on behalf of the Polish government-in-exile to bomb the rail lines to the death camps.

Told that not enough aircraft were available for that purpose, and learning at the same time of the death of his wife and child in the embattled Warsaw ghetto, Zygielbojm took an overdose of sleeping pills in his London apartment on May 12, 1943. In his suicide note Zygielbojm wrote that the "crime of murdering the entire Jewish population of Poland falls . . . on the perpetrators . . . but indirectly also it weighs on the whole of humanity." The *New York Times* published Zygielbojm's despairing letter in its entirety on June 4, 1943, under the headline "Pole's Suicide Note Pleads for Jews."

Another voice aimed at persuading the United States to take action against the wholesale killing of Jews in Eastern Europe was that of Jan Karski. In 1942 Karski, a young Polish diplomat and a Roman Catholic, entered the Warsaw ghetto disguised as a Jew and was able to report on the walled-in fortress that contained 500,000 doomed Jews trying to hold out against German might. Karski had also been successful in infiltrating a sorting station for the Nazi death camp of Belzec, near the Polish border with Ukraine.

Carrying microfilmed documents testifying to the horrors he had witnessed, Karski made his way to the United States and met with Supreme Court Justice Felix Frankfurter, himself a Jew of German background. Frankfurter's response after listening carefully to Karski, who spoke English well and had a photographic memory, was, "I don't believe you. I do not mean that you are lying. I simply said I cannot believe you."

Disbelief regarding the emaciated occupants of the Warsaw ghetto and the victims of the Belzec death camp would be understandable had the evidence come from a solitary witness. But there were also the reports of Zygielbojm. And in June 1942 the London *Daily Telegraph* published the report of the Jewish Labor Bund. In Poland alone 700,000 Jews had already been killed. Throughout Europe one million more had been murdered. The *New York Times* picked up the story but unfortunately did not see fit to headline it. It was buried in one of the back pages of the newspaper.

Despite evidence of the speed and efficacy of the Nazi killing machine, the war strategy of the Allied nations—Britain, Russia, and the United States—was to defeat Germany militarily and to worry about its crimes against humanity later. It must also be acknowledged that anti-Semitism was ingrained in all of the fighting nations; this cultural and religious prejudice had existed in many parts of the world since before the first Jewish exile from Palestine, as early as the sixth century BCE. And the diversion of aircraft to bomb rail lines leading to the death camps seemed excessive during a time of heavy ground and air battles elsewhere.

The process of naming Hitler's slaughter of the Jews as genocide would take only another year—until 1943. But recognizing it as an international crime that much of the world would condemn was to take decades.

The Nazis weren't prosecuted for war crimes until after World War II, but the atrocities they perpetrated against the Jews and other populations gave rise to the word *genocide*. Here, Nazi leaders Hermann Goering (left) and Rudolf Hess lean forward in the dock to listen to testimony against them at the Nuremberg trials.

The Persistence of Raphael Lemkin

Soghomon Tehlirian's 1921 assassination of Talaat Pasha, one of the powerful Turkish leaders behind the Armenian genocide, engaged the interest of Raphael Lemkin, a twenty-one-year-old Polish Jew. Lemkin was at the time studying linguistics at the University of Lvov in Poland. He found himself questioning Tehlirian's arrest for the crime. If it was illegal to kill one person, how great was the illegality of killing one million? Or did a sovereign state rather than an individual have the freedom to murder beyond limits?

By 1933, having attained a law degree, Lemkin already found himself an early victim of Hitler's influence on neighboring Poland. He attempted to deliver a paper he had written that called attention to the Turkish ethnic cleansing of the Armenians in 1915–1918 at an international law conference in Madrid. But the Polish government refused to let him leave the country.

His paper condemned the "Barbarity" of "the premeditated destruction of national, racial, religious, and social collectivities." "Vandalism" Lemkin defined as "the destruction of works of art and culture, being the expression of the particular genius of these collectivities." Lemkin also called attention to the dangers of the ascent of Hitler. As a result, the anti-Semitic Warsaw government fired him from his job as deputy public prosecutor.

Hitler's invasion of Poland on September 1, 1939, was the

signal for Lemkin to flee. Beset by dangers, he managed to find refuge in Sweden in early 1940 and to reach the United States in April 1941. Like Zygielbojm and Karski, Lemkin tried to contact officials in the highest government offices to persuade them to take action against the barbarities being enacted in Nazi-held Europe.

His lobbying for a treaty making the protection of minorities one of the aims of the war against Germany met with no interest from either Henry Wallace, Franklin Roosevelt's vice president, or from Roosevelt himself. The latter refused him an audience and sent Lemkin a message advising patience.

Prior to May 8, 1945, the date on which the war in Europe ended—with the deaths of 6 million Jews and 5 million Poles, Gypsies, Communists, and other "undesirables"—Lemkin had constructed his word for the barbarity that had taken place—genocide.

Lemkin hoped that the Nuremberg trials of 1945, at which Germany was prosecuted for its "crimes against humanity," would be the venue for the formulation of an international agreement leading to both the condemnation of and action against guilty nations. But, disappointingly, the Nuremberg tribunal did not take into account Hitler's crimes against Germany's Jews before the war because Germany was a sovereign state. Only Hitler's crimes in the conquered territories were placed under investigation.

But Lemkin persevered. A new international organization had been created in San Francisco in 1945—the United Nations. At that point, in 1946, the fledgling alliance of countries of the world was meeting on Long Island in New York, and Lemkin was there, determined to introduce a resolution for a law that called for international action against the crime of genocide.

To Lemkin's credit, he succeeded in interesting the United Nations in forming a subcommittee to examine and define the crime of genocide and to make it punishable under international law. The UN Convention on the Prevention and Punishment of the Crime of Genocide (CPPCG) met in Geneva, Switzerland, in 1948, and Lemkin was there to lobby the delegates of the various nations represented and to urge its ratification.

Lemkin had learned since the end of the war that close to fifty members of his family had perished, most of them in the Warsaw ghetto, in the concentration camps, or on death marches. Of his immediate family, only his older brother had survived. It was vital to Lemkin that the definition of genocide on which the CPPCG agreed should cover as many aspects as possible of this crime.

The agreed-upon definition was as follows: any of the following acts committed with intent to destroy, in whole or in part, a national, ethnical, racial, or religious group, as such:

A. killing members of the group;
B. causing serious bodily or mental harm to members of the group;
C. deliberately inflicting on the group the conditions of life calculated to bring about its physical destruction in whole or in part;
D. imposing measures intended to prevent births within the group;
E. forcibly transferring children of the group to another group.

During times of peace or war, genocide, as defined above, made national leaders, public officials, and even private citizens liable for punishment if they were responsible for attacking a targeted group, as had taken place in the case of the Armenians, the Jews, and others. Attacks on untargeted groups with no special identification were not genocide; they were defined as mass homicide and did not fall under the aegis of the United Nations' CPPCG.

Ratification of the resolution on genocide by the delegates to the subcommittee and by a number of UN member states took place readily. And in June 1949 President Harry Truman called for its ratification by the U.S. Senate, where a two-thirds vote was required for adoption. To the despair of Raphael Lemkin and many others, objections began to be raised.

How *many* individuals of a specific group had to be killed to call a situation genocide? What if it was only a very small number? Would the treatment of American Indians and African Americans by the United States be considered genocide? Would punishment be retroactive? How did a powerful nation like the United States feel about having international law infringe on *its* sovereignty? Was the United States open to the idea of responding to charges brought by other nations regarding its infractions? Hardly.

Under Truman's 1953 successor, Dwight D. Eisenhower, the battle for ratification died. Even though the troops commanded by this former World War II general had liberated Germany's Buchenwald concentration camp, the self-protective legal interests of the United States remained foremost.

In 1959 a despairing Lemkin succumbed to a heart attack. He had received a number of nominations for the Nobel Peace Prize but never received it. Nor would it be until 1988—during which time several genocides would have taken place around the world— that the United States would finally ratify the UN treaty on the crime that Raphael Lemkin named.

A female Khmer Rouge fighter carries an AK-47 assault rifle in the jungles of western Cambodia.

2 Genocide Behind a Wall of Silence: Cambodia's Killing Fields

"IT WAS THE MORNING OF APRIL 17, 1975. THE gleaming sun rose gradually, emerging from the horizon in a captivating view. In contrast, our lives little by little began to move into darkness. . . . We found ourselves hiding inside the house pretending to be unaware of any outside events. But soon we were awakened by a throng of Khmer Rouge soldiers banging on our front door. 'Go or we will shoot!'"

That day, thirteen-year-old Moly Ly and his family left their home in the Cambodian capital city of Phnom Penh. "We walked with our bundles on our shoulders and heads . . . a group of Khmer Rouge soldiers threatened the crowds, 'Go! Go! Hurry! Hurry!' . . . Our lives were gradually being claimed by these ferocious animals, the illiterate and brainwashed Khmer Rouge, whose leaders were obedient to China."

The swift cultural, political, and genocidal revolution (Cambodia's Muslims, Buddhists, and Catholics were targeted) that took hold in the Southeast Asian country of Cambodia in April 1975 was, like the Armenian and Jewish genocides earlier in the twentieth century, related to a major war. Since 1959 the United States had been involved in a war against Communist North Vietnam and in support of non-Communist South Vietnam. Fighting had overflowed into neighboring Cambodia.

In 1975 the United States withdrew from Vietnam in defeat. The Communist north had overtaken the south, and Vietnam would be reunited under a Communist government. As a result of the U.S. departure from the area, Lon Nol, the corrupt and repressive anti-Communist head of state of Cambodia whom the Americans had been backing, also fled.

This turn of events gave the Khmer Rouge (Red Cambodians) the opportunity to take control of Cambodia that they had long been waiting for. Their leaders had been schooled in the extremist Communist ideology of Mao Zedong, a founder of the Chinese Communist Party and, in 1949, leader of the People's Republic of China. Mao's theories reinterpreted those of Communism's founders—Karl Marx and Vladimir Lenin—to elevate the importance of the peasantry—the masses of food growers, obedient and hardworking, who formed the basis of society. China was ideologically but not militarily involved in the Red Cambodian takeover.

During the Cultural Revolution, which peaked in 1966–1969 in China, Communist leader Mao Zedong attempted to bring back the "classless" society of the early days of the revolution. He placed authority in the hands of a group of young soldiers known as the Red Guards. The Red Guards were empowered to denounce and attack intellectuals, university professors, scientists, artists, and anyone else they decided to label a "class enemy." Universities were closed, and foreign culture was banned. Public ridicule of the accused led to suicides. Jailing and constant hounding led to thousands of deaths.

It was from this aspect of Maoist thought that the Khmer Rouge drew their ideas for the governance of Cambodia once the American bombing had ceased and peace seemed to be at hand. The Khmer Kingdom, a nineteenth-century protectorate of France that was once a powerful empire and most recently a wartime enemy of the United States, was about to experience one of the most vicious assaults on humanity that the world had ever seen. Under the new name Democratic Kampuchea, the country would experience 2 million people being shot, bludgeoned, tortured, and worked and starved to death within the space of three and a half years, mainly for cultural and political reasons, but also for their religious adherence to Islam, Buddhism, or Christianity.

Reviewing the unbridled barbarism of the killings in Cambodia, the following question has been asked by historians and other observers: Would the Khmer Rouge have been so brutal in their attack on society if the American bombings of the preceding years had not been so intense? The tonnage dropped on Cambodia by the United States (more than 500,000) was three times greater than had been dropped on Japan in World War II, including the two atom bombs.

The question remains unresolved. In terrifying the Cambodian peasantry and sending many of them to live in shantytowns on

In this photo taken outside of Cambodia, China's chairman Mao Zedong (left) greets Khmer Rouge official Ieng Sary (right) as Khmer Rouge leader Pol Pot looks on.

the outskirts of cities, the U.S. air assaults may have augmented the ranks of the Khmer Rouge. Who were the men in ill-fitting black uniforms and Chinese Mao caps driving around in jeeps in Phnom Penh on the morning of April 17, 1975?

Most of them had been recruited from the poorest regions of the countryside, where they lived without running water or electricity, without schools, without any form of money, without automotive vehicles or even roads. Their farming implements were crude handmade hoes, spades, and axes. Under the tutelage of the Khmer leaders, they had learned to despise the cities, especially the sophisticated capital of Phnom Penh, where intellectuals, educators, and wealthy businessmen lived. They were taught to view the cities as places of evil in which capitalism thrived.

Their initial orders were that Phnom Penh be evacuated. On entering the homes of the city dwellers forced to leave at gunpoint, the Khmer recruits were astonished by refrigerators and modern sanitary equipment. "Soldiers drank water from toilet bowls, thinking they were what city people used instead of wells . . . others ate toothpaste."

They vandalized furnishings, commandeered motorbikes and automobiles, which they promptly drove into trees or buildings, broke into shops, and destroyed valuable goods. Many of the newly recruited troops were teenagers, even children of eleven or twelve, armed with burdensome AK-47 machine guns.

But the material destruction in the city was nothing compared with the fate that awaited the city dwellers. On that afternoon of April 17, the inhabitants were told that the Americans were about to bomb the city and that they would be able to return in two or three days. Both pieces of information were untrue. Instead, some 600,000 longtime city dwellers, as well as about 2 million refugees from the American bombing, found themselves on the crowded roads heading north out of the capital.

"It was a stupefying sight, a human flood pouring out of the

Survivors sifted through the rubble after the Khmer Rouge bombed Phnom Penh.

city . . . bicycles overflowing with bundles, and others behind little home-made carts. Most were on foot." The Khmer Rouge ordered the city's hospitals, housing 15,000 to 20,000 people at the time, to be emptied immediately. "Sick people were left by their families at the roadside. Others were killed [by the soldiers] because they could walk no further. Children who had lost their parents cried out in tears. . . . The dead were abandoned, covered in flies, sometimes with a piece of cloth thrown over them. Women gave birth wherever they could."

The leader who was to take control of Cambodia after April 1975 and to direct the murderous regime that was to follow was a previously little-known member of the Communist Party of Kampuchea (CPK) and a former schoolteacher by the name of Saloth Sar. Believing that disguise was the best protection against one's enemies, Sar had many aliases. But the name that would make him as notorious and universally despised as Adolf Hitler was Pol Pot.

The Rise of the Infamous Pol Pot

Unlike the Khmer Rouge soldiers that he was later to incite toward the attainment of a classless Communist society, the man eventually known as Pol Pot was born the son of a relatively prosperous rice farmer, probably in 1925. Like his brothers, Sar, as he was then known, was educated, first at a Buddhist monastery for a year, and then—at the age of ten—at a school run by French Catholic priests in Phnom Penh.

In the 1930s the Cambodian capital was a cosmopolitan city, inhabited by French, Chinese, and Vietnamese, who controlled the country's government and its commercial life. It was also the site of the royal palace, where Sar's sister was a concubine of the king and whom he visited from time to time. As the future Pol Pot, Sar would abolish all forms of education, all religions, and of course deny the claims of the onetime monarchy.

World War II and the invasion of France by Hitler's forces weakened French power in what was then known as Indochina, consisting of Vietnam, Laos, and Cambodia. As early as 1946 Vietnamese Communist forces began their attack on the French to oust them from the region. Cambodia, however, was still not ready to revolt against France. In fact, Sar, having completed his higher technical school studies, was awarded a scholarship to an engineering school in France.

Arriving in Paris in 1949, Sar soon underwent a political transformation. He joined a movement to free Cambodia from French control and to rid it of its ruler, Prince Norodom

Sihanouk, and became a member of the French Communist Party. At the time he took much of his radical inspiration from the instigators of the French Revolution. Like Cambodia in the 1950s, France in the late 1700s had been a feudal, preindustrial country. Sar saw the abolition of private property and the creation of an egalitarian society as his true revolutionary goal for Cambodia.

Years were to pass before conditions were right for Sar's emergence as Pol Pot, the driving force behind the Cambodian genocide. During that period he returned to Cambodia (in 1953) and joined a Vietnamese Communist guerrilla base camp in the Cambodian forest east of Phnom Penh.

A few years later Sar returned to Phnom Penh, where he married and lived a double life, teaching history and French literature, while simultaneously holding meetings in safe houses where he indoctrinated students and colleagues into his Communist ideals. Although France had granted independence to Cambodia in 1953, Prince Sihanouk was still in power and was clamping down on rebel activities.

Once more, in 1963, Sar went into hiding in the jungle wilderness, where he would direct military operations against the government and bide his time. In 1966, when the Cultural Revolution erupted in China, Sar declared, "organisationally and ideologically our people are ready . . . to launch a true people's war," and he hailed Mao Zedong as "the great, guiding star who brings unceasing victories."

When the time was finally ripe for Sar to strike—after the overthrow of the monarchy in 1970 and the hurried departure of the Americans in 1975—all the pent-up energies of the renamed Pol Pot swept the nation. The American bombing had killed 500,000 Cambodians; Pol Pot would murder 2 million (of a population of 7 million).

The Cambodian Killing Fields

Bewildered evacuees driven out of Phnom Penh and other cities, bearing little more than the few possessions they could wheel or carry, were told they were headed for safety. Their destinations were actually the various zones throughout the country where rural life predominated and where rice growing was the main occupation.

In these agricultural hinterlands, private property and owner-ship of material goods would not exist. The national goal set by Pol Pot and the members of the Communist Party of Kampuchea (CPK) was increased farm production. To this end the "new" people arriving from the cities (some 600,000 from Phnom Penh alone) were required to join the "old" or "base" people native to the region in laboring long hours in the rice fields, not only to grow rice but to dig irrigation ditches that were intended in time to increase the harvests.

Life as the new people had known it was stripped down to its barest essentials. They lived and ate in communes under the watch-ful eyes of Khmer Rouge village militias that included both men and women. Like their overseers, the new people wore black, but they were permitted no colorful scarves or other adornments; no watches, radios, cameras, books, or currency. Former doctors, law-yers, educators, university students, civil servants, and even persons who wore eyeglasses, and were thus considered intellectuals, were put under constant surveillance for remarks or behavior disloyal to Angkar, the faceless leadership that ran Democratic Kampuchea.

Angkar can be loosely translated as "the Organization" or "Big Brother." At the lowest level Angkar (not to be confused with Angkor Wat, the renowned, richly carved temple of the ancient Khmer Empire in northwestern Cambodia) was the village committee that held autonomy over the lives of the recently arrived rice-field laborers and could order an on-the-spot execution with the blow of an axe or a hoe handle at any time.

At the highest level Angkar was Pol Pot and the other national leaders. After confessing to past sins, such as loyalty to the former Cambodian regime, a suspect from the cities could be sent away for "reeducation," never to reappear.

The overseers of the communes varied in the severity of the punishments they doled out. Some were stony-faced, others capricious and unpredictable. Most were illiterate and predisposed toward anger at the former city dwellers. A frequently punished crime was the search for food to supplement the minimal daily ration of rice. People who were caught eating grass, crickets, grasshoppers, snails, frogs, snakes, and rats to supplement their near-starvation diets were liable to be put to death.

Starvation was a major cause of natural death, as were diseases such as malaria and dysentery, among the new people. Modern medicine was abandoned, and those unable to work were neither treated nor fed. The work week, as it was in the days of the French Revolution, consisted of ten days, with one day off.

Angkar abolished the concept of paying wages, along with money and markets for the purpose of purchasing food, clothing, and other necessities. Food, clothing, and shelter were supplied by the state, which was, in effect, a slave state, in which human beings were viewed as little more than oxen. When a person was to be killed for violating the rules of the commune, the view of the local leaders was "To keep you is no profit, to destroy you is no loss." An overall indifference to human life was expressed through Red Cambodia's various forms of cultural, class, and religious genocide.

Family life was another aspect of normalcy that was sacrificed to Angkar. Starting in the summer of 1976, children were taken away from their parents at the age of seven so that they could be indoctrinated with the teachings of the revolution and sent to work in the fields. Schools for elementary learning had been abolished for the time being.

Spouses, too, were often separated and sent to different areas of the country to work. Marriage and the birth of children, however, were encouraged in order to increase the human labor supply. Existing marriages were sometimes ignored by the authorities, for it was Angkar that selected the mates and conducted the marriages, usually of ten or fifteen couples at one time.

While the genocide inflicted by Pol Pot and his comrades can be seen as the destruction of one segment of Cambodian culture by another, there were also groups within Cambodia that were targeted because of their religion. Buddhist and Catholic books were burned in Phnom Penh, and the practice of both religions was prohibited. Cambodian Muslims, known as Chams, after the eastern region of Cambodia that many inhabited, were forbidden to wear Islamic dress, keep their own customs, marry among themselves, and worship in their mosques. Khmer policy broke down the cultural solidarity of the Cham Muslims by dispersing them throughout the countryside.

Back in the evacuated capital of Phnom Penh, which Pol Pot entered victoriously but quietly on April 20, 1975, signs of plunder lay everywhere. The few inhabitants, mainly the sick or elderly, who had refused or been unable to leave, were eliminated on sight. "Along the roadside, cars lay abandoned and stripped, dozens and dozens of them, with their doors and windows open. . . . The houses, too, had gaping black openings. . . . In the courtyards and on the pavements, crockery, cooking stoves, fridges, lay scattered."

After killing off any former army personnel or civil servants of the government of Prince Sihanouk, Pol Pot and Cambodia's new leaders took over the administrative buildings that formerly housed them. The prince was permitted to remain in his palace but in much-reduced circumstances, akin to house arrest. He was given a tour in late 1975 of the regions to the north and east of Phnom Penh. He later wrote, "[It] bowled me over. . . . My people . . . had been transformed into cattle. . . . My eyes were opened to a madness which neither I nor anyone else had imagined."

A Cambodian boy stands in front of a platform covered with human skulls at a killing field that was not discovered until twenty years after the devastation wreaked by Pol Pot's regime.

Aside from Pol Pot's contacts with the Chinese Communist hierarchy, Cambodia had become a closed-off nation operating behind a wall of silence. There were no news reports, no foreign communications, and no flights into or out of the country. In keeping with his penchant for secrecy and apparent modesty, Pol Pot did not even take the title of prime minister until 1976, after Prince Sihanouk, horrified by the Khmer Rouge regime, abdicated in April of that year. He sought refuge mainly in China, returning to Cambodia in 1979 to support the weak anti-Vietnamese faction that remained after the takeover. In 2004 Prince Sihanouk went into permanent exile in Beijing.

Within a twelve- to eighteen-month period, Pol Pot believed he had created the ideal Communist state. He boasted that the CPK had taken the principles of Karl Marx and Vladimir Lenin and achieved a new and better form of Communism than that of other totalitarian nations, one that would make Kampuchea strong and preserve it forever. Its hardworking peasant class was becoming the foundation of the national economy—selfless, productive, and pledged to the ideology of the Khmer Rouge leaders.

There was, however, one aspect of Pol Pot's revolution that he would share with the Soviet Union's Communist regime in particular—suspicion of the loyalty and ambitious motives of one's comrades and fellow leaders, resulting in widespread purges. Pol Pot's examination of those he viewed as betraying the revolution or as personal enemies began as early as the first half of 1976.

For the purpose of extracting confessions from this group of mainly upper-echelon political prisoners, he set up the interrogation centers around the country that were to become notorious. The largest of these centers was located in an abandoned high school in Phnom Penh and was known as Tuol Sleng, code-named S-21.

The
Tuol Sleng
Torture Center

Violence, well known to Pol Pot and the Communist leadership, flourished in the rural regions. Local leaders did not hesitate to slit open the belly of a pregnant woman and hang her fetus by the neck or to extract the liver of a newly executed person for use as human food.

Despite these practices, designed as fierce warnings to those who failed to serve Angkar as required, there were indications early on that the revolution was not producing the results in either Communist zeal or ever-increasing rice production (Cambodia's principal crop) that Pol Pot's plans had called for. To address these indications of failure, Pol Pot began to round up political personnel with the aim of extracting confessions of wrongdoing, punishable by death. Tuol Sleng was known to have "processed" 16,000 people, of which only a handful survived.

Chances of release were almost nil, because condemnation came even without proof. Nonetheless, the prisoners were subjected to strict rules of behavior in answering questions and were routinely tortured with electric shocks, seared with hot metal rods, beaten on the soles of the feet, and suspended from hooks with their heads submerged in water. But death did not come easily. The orders were that as many confessions as possible were to be obtained before executions were to take place.

Among the confessions that the Khmer Rouge authorities were seeking—and that they would then record as justification for the extermination of the prisoners—were connections with such hostile nations as the United States, the Soviet Union, and Vietnam. Although the Communist Vietnamese who had infiltrated Cambodia in the early days had gone on to nurture the growth of that country's Communist movement, Pol Pot now repudiated their influence. He had become paranoid and hostile regarding Cambodia's neighbor to the east. The behavior of Pol Pot in purging his deputy corevolutionists was indeed more typical of the Soviet Union's Stalin than of Nazi Germany's Hitler.

Similarly, Tuol Sleng prisoners who were tortured to the point of confessing membership in the KGB, the Soviet Union's spy organization, were doomed to die, especially after being forced to falsely utter a sufficient number of names of other guilty parties. Having backed the Vietnamese Communists, the Soviets were seen as enemies of the Chinese, who had supported the Cambodian revolutionists. Forced confessions of working for the American spy organization, the CIA, were also, of course, a death sentence.

The confession files of the Tuol Sleng prisoners have been preserved, as have some five thousand photographs of men, women, and children of unproven guilt arriving at what was to be their final destination. Their portraits can still be seen at the Tuol Sleng Genocide Museum in Phnom Penh.

The Collapse of the Khmer Rouge

Throughout 1977 operations at Tuol Sleng continued unrelentingly, stripping Pol Pot's government of many officials in the top ranks of the CPK. Regional and local leaders, too, went to their deaths after numerous forced confessions, which took place at interrogation centers located around the country. As a result, leaders on all levels had to be shifted around or replaced with increasing frequency.

In an effort to save the failing system that the Khmer Rouge had established in 1975, in 1978 Pol Pot began to allow a few more individual freedoms. The Cambodian people were not compelled to wear only black. They were permitted to add some color to their clothing. Individual cooking, as opposed to compulsory communal meals, was permitted, and people who foraged for frogs, snakes, and other field animals to supplement their near-starvation rice diets were not punished with death. For the first time "new" people and "old" or "base" people were permitted to intermarry, and children were given a smattering of elementary schooling in some localities.

The Khmer Rouge even permitted the first American journalists to enter the country since the evacuation of Phnom Penh on April 17, 1975. They were Elizabeth Becker of the *Washington Post* and Richard Dudman of the *St. Louis Post-Dispatch*. Accompanying the two reporters was a Scotsman named Malcolm Caldwell, who was known to be a Khmer Rouge sympathizer.

Angkar spokespeople guided the visitors, showing them only a clean-swept main boulevard in Phnom Penh and keeping the rubble of the deserted homes and shops out of sight. Becker later wrote, "There were no food-stalls, no families, no young people playing sports, even sidewalk games, no one out on a walk, not even dogs or cats . . . ."

Near the end of the two-week trip, which had included a sanitized visit to the countryside and an interview with Pol Pot that was more like a tirade concerning the threat of an invasion by Vietnam, the Scotsman Malcolm Caldwell was mysteriously murdered. The two journalists returned to Beijing on the Chinese airline that had flown them into Phnom Penh (the only airline that had landing rights in Cambodia) with a casket containing the deceased Caldwell.

Fear and loathing of the Communist Vietnamese had been building among the Khmer Rouge for some years. Border skirmishes conducted by both Cambodia and Vietnam increased during 1978, resulting in the Vietnamese setting up training camps within Vietnam for Khmer refugees. And on December 25, 1978, the Vietnamese launched a full-fledged attack, sending 120,000 well-armed troops into southeastern Cambodia. By January 7, 1979, the enemy had taken Phnom Penh.

After seeing that all remaining prisoners at Tuol Sleng were exterminated, Pol Pot fled to Thailand by helicopter. There had been no time, however, to destroy the archives of the deadly interrogation center. Nor had Pol Pot's hopes for support from China against the Soviet-dominated Communists of Vietnam been adequate to prevent the takeover of so much Cambodian territory.

For a decade Pol Pot hovered in the jungle wilderness on Cambodia's northern border with Thailand or inside Thailand, hoping to gather sufficient military strength to drive the Vietnamese out of the country entirely. Meanwhile the Khmer Rouge refugees, having renounced the CPK (their Cambodian Communist party affiliation), formed a coalition government with the occupying Vietnamese.

At last the wall of silence that had encircled Cambodia from 1975 to early 1979 had been breached. Even the Vietnamese, well acquainted with the savagery of war, were shocked at the mass graves of the Cambodian killing fields—giant earthen saucers from which huge quantities of bones and skulls protruded.

Yet the United States, still smarting from its defeat in Vietnam and opposing that nation's UN legitimacy, supported the claim of the vastly reduced Khmer Rouge government to maintain its seat in the United Nations. Nor did the UN member states that had signed the treaty calling for the Prevention and Punishment of the Crime of Genocide (the United States was not yet among the signers) file charges against the Khmer Rouge at the International Court of Justice. The member states simply looked the other way in spite of a UN final report that condemned Cambodia's crimes as "the most serious that had occurred anywhere in the world since Nazism."

Even among the Khmer Rouge leaders there were many who escaped punishment. Pol Pot, principal among them, was never brought to trial. He died in relative comfort of a heart attack in April 1998, at the age of approximately seventy-three. But three decades after the 1979 defeat of the Khmer Rouge regime in Cambodia, a UN–backed trial had finally gotten under way. During the 2009 hearings a handful of survivors of Tuol Sleng prison were able to bring charges against five of their torturers. Results are forthcoming.

A Hutu man takes cover as the Rwandan Patriotic Front rebels fire at Rwandan soldiers.

3 Genocide in Rwanda: Tutsi Slaughter by the Hutu

"DECIMATE"—IT NOT ONLY MEANS "TO DESTROY IN large part," it also means "to kill every tenth person in a group." That is what happened in the tiny, east-central African nation of Rwanda in a mere one hundred days in the spring and summer of 1994.

An estimated 800,000 people of a population of 8 million were shot, blown up with grenades, or more commonly hacked to death with machetes, knives, bamboo spears, or the traditional Rwandan *masu*—a club from which nails protrude. When these weapons were not available, the killers used "screwdrivers, hammers, and bicycle handlebars." They even made knives out of the sharpened leaf springs of demolished automobiles.

Who were the killers, who were the victims, and what was the root cause of the genocide that flared up within Rwanda's borders? In the sixteenth century the Hutu of the region, a Bantu people who inhabited much of central and southern Africa, were invaded by the Tutsi, a northern people said to have originated in Ethiopia.

Soon the Hutu, who were in the majority, were being ruled by a series of Tutsi kings known as *mwamis*. While the Hutu were traditional farmers, the Tutsi were herdsmen, many made wealthy and powerful through their ownership of cattle. There were said to be differences, too, in the physical features of the two groups. The Tutsi tended to be tall and lanky, with elongated heads and thin noses, while the Hutu were stocky, broad-faced, and flat-nosed. The Hutu were also identified as being darker skinned than the Tutsi.

The two groups spoke the same language—Kinyarwanda, were followers of the same religion, and intermarried with the passage of years, so that the so-called distinct physical types had begun to merge.

From the late 1800s until just after World War I, present-day Rwanda was part of German East Africa. Following Germany's defeat in the war, the colony was mandated to Belgium, which became its next colonial master. Although the Tutsi kings continued to rule, the Belgians saw fit in the 1930s to issue ethnic identity cards, distinguishing the Tutsi minority from the Hutu majority. The purpose appeared to be mainly administrative.

Change came with the abolition of the Rwandan monarchy in 1961 and Rwandan independence from Belgium in 1962. Even earlier, in 1959, the Hutu majority had supported a dictatorial Hutu president and had deposed the Tutsi rulers. As a result, 150,000 Tutsi fled to the small neighboring nation of Burundi, where a Tutsi military regime was in place. Most Tutsis, however, remained in Rwanda.

Hutu majority rule offered long-sought satisfaction to the nearly 85 percent of the population that had once been ruled by Tutsi kings. In the new republic, however, there was to be a power-sharing arrangement, which would permit both groups to live in harmony. But peaceful relations between them had not existed for three decades. By 1990 refugee Tutsis in neighboring Uganda had formed the Rwandan Patriotic Front (RPF) and were making sporadic attacks on Hutus in Rwanda. Meanwhile, Hutu Youth militias and the Hutu Power movement within Rwanda were training for war and stockpiling weapons.

In 1993, concerned western powers and the African country of Tanzania initiated peace talks in the Tanzanian city of Arusha. Under the so-called Arusha Accords, Rwanda's leaders agreed that moderate Hutu parties and Tutsi opposition parties would participate in the government. There would also be a peace agreement between the Hutu president, Juvénal Habyarimana, and the Tutsi RPF.

To preside over the peace agreement, the United Nations sent a peacekeeping force to Rwanda to patrol the cease-fire. The multinational UN Assistance Mission in Rwanda (UNAMIR) was under the command of a Canadian military officer, Lieutenant General Roméo Dallaire. UNAMIR's assignment did not permit the discharge of arms unless its members were directly attacked. But it was felt that the presence of 2,500 blue-helmeted UN soldiers from Belgium, Bangladesh, Ghana, Tunisia, and twenty other countries would prove effective in preserving the goals of the Arusha Accords. The UN presence would be shown to be entirely inadequate in a nation of 8 million.

Peace Fails Once Again

As soon as Lieutenant General Dallaire and his UNAMIR force arrived in Rwanda, late in 1993, the commander became aware of how little attention was being paid to the high-minded Arusha Accords. Through a secret informant he learned that Hutu Power extremists had drawn up lists of Tutsis living in the Rwandan capital of Kigali who were to be slain in the first onslaught.

In addition, the Hutu, who had been importing guns from France and machetes from China, had major arms caches hidden throughout the country. The Hutu also planned to murder as many of the 440 well-prepared Belgian peacekeepers as possible in order to get that country's contingent to leave Rwanda. Nor was the rest of UNAMIR welcome in Hutu-controlled Rwanda. The peacekeeping force was seen as an accomplice of the Tutsi minority.

Lieutenant General Roméo Dallaire poses in front of a United Nations jeep bearing the flag that accompanied him during his tour of duty in Rwanda.

A Rwandan rebel fighter walks by the plane wreckage in Kigali in which Rwanda's president Juvénal Habyarimana died.

Dallaire was still petitioning the United Nations for more and better-supplied peacekeepers and for permission to perform arms sweeps in Rwanda when the event that catalyzed the genocide took place. On April 6, 1994, the private jet of Hutu president Habyarimana, who was returning from a meeting in Tanzania, was shot down by ground-fired missiles as it approached the Kigali airport. In the plane along with Habyarimana were several high-level aides and the recently elected president of Burundi, Cyprien Ntaryamira. All those aboard were killed.

The question of who was responsible for the president's murder would never be fully resolved. Were those who downed the plane Hutu extremists or Tutsi oppositionists? As events unfolded, it appeared more and more likely that the attackers had been hard-line Hutus seeking license to begin the bloody elimination of moderate Hutus (those who favored power sharing) and of all Tutsis in Rwanda.

Among the very first official victims, killed on April 7, was the prime minister of Rwanda, Agathe Uwilingiyimana, a Hutu moderate who had automatically become head of state following the president's death. Although Dallaire's UNAMIR force tried to protect Uwilingiyimana from the Hutu raid on her home, she was murdered by members of the Rwandan army.

Nor did the Hutu-targeted Belgian soldiers of UNAMIR escape the fate that had been planned for them. Ten Belgians were separated from the peacekeeping force, were tortured and killed, and their bodies mutilated. As a result, all Belgian soldiers were withdrawn from Rwanda, as were most other foreign nationals, especially Americans and Europeans. Rwandans who worked for white foreigners, ranging from office assistants to family domestics, pleaded to be taken out of the country, to no avail.

The Presidential Guards took command of the very early killing. Under direct orders from such hard-liners as Army Staff Director Colonel Théoneste Bagosora, they set up roadblocks to drag Tutsis from their cars and surrounded hospitals and churches in search of refuge-seekers. The killings also spread rapidly into the hands of the Hutu militia known as the Interahamwe ("those who attack together"). The militias, which included the Hutu Youth, were all part of an organized Hutu Power movement that had long been training for the onslaught and that possessed hidden caches of weapons. The Hutu militia's killing frenzy quickly incited ordinary citizens, who were encouraged to use whatever weaponry was at hand, to destroy their Tutsi neighbors. The existence of the identity cards that all Rwandans carried helped the Hutu attackers to find their victims.

Having long given up their traditional religion, 65 percent of Rwandans were Catholic and about 15 percent Protestant. Churches thus became places of refuge as both roaming Hutu militias and local citizens pursued the Tutsis in a given area. But priests and pastors soon learned that they had no power to protect those who sought shelter. Other clergy were even complicit in the killings of Tutsi refugees, likely seeking their own immunity from the Hutu Power attackers.

At one church run by Polish missionaries, Dallaire's executive assistant Brent Beardsley "found 150 people, dead mostly, though some were still groaning, who had been attacked the night before. The Polish priests told us it had been incredibly well organized. The Rwandan army had cleared out the area, the gendarmerie had rounded up all the Tutsi, and the militia had hacked them to death."

School buildings were not immune to the violence. Beardsley reported that at a school across the street from the church, "there were children, I don't know how many, forty, sixty, eighty children stacked up outside who had all been chopped up with machetes. Some of their mothers had heard them screaming and had come running, and the militia had killed them, too."

The only largely successful stand against the butchery that was decimating the population of Rwanda throughout the months of

The courageous stand of Paul Rusesabagina, who saved 1,200 people at his hotel, was memorialized in the film *Hotel Rwanda.*

April, May, and June of 1994 was that taken by a courageous Hutu, Paul Rusesabagina. As the manager of a large, foreign-owned hotel in Rwanda, he found himself able to save more than 1,200 people through a combination of shrewdness and daring.

The Horror Within and the World Outside

For the vast majority of Rwanda's Tutsis and moderate Hutus, death was almost a certainty. As one would-be victim, a lawyer named Laurent Nkongoli, put it, "I had accepted death. At a certain moment this happens. One hopes not to die cruelly, but one expects to die anyway. Not death by machete, one hopes, but with a bullet. If you were willing to pay for it, you could often ask for a bullet."

What happened to the piles of bodies of those who had been chopped to death by government soldiers, by the roaming militias, by their very own neighbors? The rapidity of their accumulation

The Hôtel des Mille Collines

Although Rwanda had received its independence from Belgium in 1962, Belgian commercial interests were still operating in the country at the time of the genocide in 1994. Paul Rusesabagina, a Rwandan Hutu, had worked since 1984 at two Kigali luxury hotels owned by Sabena, the Belgian airline.

On April 9, two days after the slaughter in Kigali had begun, Rusesabagina was informed that, as director-general of the Hôtel des Diplomates, he was under orders to hand over the hotel to Colonel Bagosora, whose "interim government" planned to use it as a headquarters. Rusesabagina, his family, and a number of friends and neighbors immediately left their homes and found themselves installed as prisoners of the new government in the hotel that he had been managing since 1993. He staved off attempts to kill members of his entourage by handing out great sums of money. How long, though, could this tactic last?

Three days later, on April 12, an amazing turn of events took place. The mercurial Colonel Bagosora decided that the new headquarters was too accessible a target for the Tutsi raiders of the RPF and arranged for his company to flee Kigali for a more obscure command post. At the same time Rusesabagina received a message from the Dutch manager of the hotel at which he had worked from 1984 to 1992— the Hôtel des Mille Collines (named for Rwanda's "thousand hills"). As a foreign national, the manager was preparing to leave the country without delay. Could Rusesabagina take over for him?

After packing some thirty of his people into a hotel van, Rusesabagina followed the government convoy of armored vehicles as ordered. Then, as the Hôtel des Mille Collines approached, he craftily turned his vehicle onto the entry road. During the months that followed, the international business-class hotel, vacated by guests from abroad and even foreign journalists, became a sanctuary for Hutu oppositionists and for Tutsis, including orphaned children, women, and the elderly.

The hotel's $125-per-night rooms became the homes of groups of refugees of all ages and backgrounds, while Rusesabagina cajoled, pandered to, and bribed the ever-threatening army and Interahamwe units whose aim was to seize his "guests."

Children were among the choice victims of the Hutu killers, for the Hutu had vowed to prevent a future generation of Tutsi. And at least 250,000 Tutsi women were said to have been raped during the genocide. Cash from the hotel safe, liquor from its cellars, and Cuban cigars were among the payoffs made to the corrupt unit commanders who visited frequently to collect their prizes.

With the help of UNAMIR, Paul Rusesabagina made a first attempt to evacuate a portion of the hotel's refugees to safety on May 3, 1994. But Hutu roadblocks forced them to turn back. The threat of the Tutsi RPF in exile to execute Hutu government prisoners that they were holding provided a bargaining chip that led to a first successful evacuation on May 27. The last of the 1,200 survivors left Rwanda on June 18.

made it impossible for morgues and cemeteries to accommodate them. Often they lay as they fell, causing the dog population of Rwanda to grow until the Tutsi RPF took over the country in the late summer of 1994 and began shooting the scavenging animals.

The horror that was taking place in Rwanda was not a secret. Unlike the Cambodian genocide, which had operated behind a wall of silence, the country was not cut off from communication with the outside world. Paul Rusesabagina was in frequent contact by telephone with the directors of Sabena Airlines in Belgium. Josh Hammer, a *Newsweek* correspondent who briefly stayed at the Hôtel des Mille Collines in mid-April, reported seeing a gang of Interahamwe running in the street. He stated, "You could literally see the blood dripping off their clubs and machetes."

Yet, aside from the small UNAMIR force of Lieutenant General Dallaire, the International Red Cross, and Médecins Sans Frontiéres (Doctors Without Borders), no foreign nation or other outside force intervened during the worst of the one hundred days of killing. In fact, on April 21, just as Lieutenant General Dallaire was pleading for a doubling of UNAMIR to 5,000 and a free hand to use arms against the Hutu killers, the United Nations slashed the size of the force to only 270 troops (although Dallaire managed through steady persuasion to keep 503).

Already on April 9 and 10 the U.S. embassy in Kigali had been closed and 250 Americans plus the ambassador and his staff had been evacuated. Rwandan embassy employees were refused sanctuary, and 35 were killed. The situation was the same with regard to other foreign missions in Rwanda. One of the bluntest remarks regarding the American departure came from Senate minority leader Bob Dole. "I don't think we have any national interest there. The Americans are out, and as far as I'm concerned, in Rwanda, that ought to be the end of it."

What had happened to the pledge that so many nations had made by ratifying the UN's 1948 Convention on the Prevention and Punishment of the Crime of Genocide (CPPCG)? After four decades of deliberation, the United States had finally, in 1988, joined with other nations in condemning and vowing to punish this crime against humanity. Of course, before any action could be taken, the crime had to be clearly defined as genocide. The question, however, of *who* decides a crime is genocide remained unanswered.

The administration of President Bill Clinton began to examine the killings in Rwanda. For two months, while hundreds of thousands of Rwandans perished, the U.S. State Department questioned the nature of the conflict. Were the perpetrators attacking an ethnic group? Yes. Was the purpose of the perpetrators to physically destroy the group in whole or in part? Yes. Were the perpetrators trying to wipe out the next generation of the ethnic group? Yes.

Yet the investigative spokesperson for the State Department was reluctant to use the word "genocide" with reference to Rwanda, lest the United States be forced to take military action to halt the killing. Only "acts of genocide" were being committed, according to the spokesperson's muddied conclusion. Not until June 10, 1994, did Secretary of State Warren Christopher hesitantly state, "If there is any particular magic in calling it genocide, I have no hesitancy in saying that."

The Rwanda of July 1994 was a scene of widespread devastation. The nation's infrastructure had been heavily damaged. Water supplies had been disrupted, and electricity was scarce. Houses had been looted and vehicles destroyed. Untended crops had ripened and were rotting in the fields, where the refugee Tutsi—now moving back into the country—would graze their cattle.

At this point the United States came forward with some humanitarian aid for both the Hutu refugees in Zaire, dying of hunger and cholera, and for those Rwandans struggling to renew their lives inside the country. But this seemed trivial compared to the assistance that could have been given even without a military intervention. The United States could have backed UNAMIR and

The United States Ignores Rwanda, and France Intervenes

Would the United States have intervened if the Rwandan genocide had taken six months or a year instead of a mere hundred days? Were the Hutu attackers too fast for America, a signatory to the genocide prevention convention (CPPCG), to react? All that is known is that not a single top-level foreign policy meeting on the subject of military intervention was held in Washington during the entire three months of the slaughter.

Meanwhile, Rwanda continued to be represented at the United Nations, at the time holding one of the rotating seats on the Security Council. As Samantha Power, author of *A Problem from Hell*, points out, "Neither the United States nor any other UN member state ever suggested that the representative of the genocidal government be expelled from the council."

Although individual members of Congress, the press, and other public media alluded frequently to the shameful indifference of the United States toward the horrors taking place in Rwanda, the Clinton administration remained firm in its conviction that intervention was not actually mandated under the CPPCG; the treaty only "enabled" intervention.

When a foreign military force did finally arrive in Rwanda, it came late in the conflict and from an unexpected source—France. The European nation then led by President François Mitterand had long had a military and political interest in the regime of the slain Hutu president, Juvénal Habyarimana. In fact, the private jet in which Habyarimana had lost his life had been a gift from the president of France.

Was Opération Turquoise, as the intervention was called, an effort to make amends for the pro-Hutu, anti-Tutsi stand of the French? If so, how effective was it? The intervention force arrived on June 23, 1994, only weeks before the Tutsi Rwandan Patriotic Front (RPF) had taken sufficient control of Rwanda to be sworn in as its new government.

France's operation consisted of 2,500 men armed with great firepower for what was intended to be a largely humanitarian intervention. Although Opération Turquoise was purported to have a neutral purpose and to save as many Tutsi lives as possible, it was wildly cheered by the Interahamwe and actually put some of the RPF then approaching victory in danger.

On July 4 Kigali fell to the Tutsi rebels; by July 14 the remnants of the Hutu interim government were fast disintegrating; and on July 19 the RPF took over as the official leader of a ravaged Rwanda. The French soon left, exaggeratingly declaring that they had been responsible for saving tens of thousands of lives. At the same time the tragic aftermath of the genocide began to unfold. Despite the promise that this time there would be a *real* power-sharing government, as many as 1.7 million Hutu refugees fled Rwanda, headed mainly for camps in neighboring Zaire and Tanzania.

could have influenced the United Nations to give General Dallaire the troop strength he needed.

The Clinton administration could have been early and forth-coming in identifying the crime as genocide and in using its powers to denounce the interim government of Rwanda and threaten its leaders with retribution. Late in 1994 the UN Security Council set up a war crimes tribunal for Rwanda, but by that time it was too late for a single life to be saved.

On March 25, 1998, President Clinton visited Rwanda and made an apology that was long overdue. "We in the United States and the world community did not do as much as we could have and should have done to try to limit what occurred. . . . Never again must we be shy in the face of evidence."

Clinton's remorseful words were surely genuine as he looked back at the 800,000 dead of Rwanda. But how would they play out with regard to future genocides? For, sadly, there would be more to come.

In July 2005, former president Bill Clinton traveled to Kigali, Rwanda, to pay tribute to the victims of Rwandan genocide.

4 Genocide in the Former Yugoslavia: Destroying Bosnia's Muslims

"Two hundred Serb paramilitaries entered the [Bosnian] village while others blocked the entrances and exits. House by house they ordered the people out into the main street. The men were separated from the women and children; and the women and children, after being robbed of their money and jewellery [sic], were allowed to go . . . while their homes were looted, blown up, or burned. The men—180 of them—were taken to the village primary school, and held there for two days. . . . Their fate was never discovered."

During the summer and fall of 1992, 70,000 Bosnian Muslims, mainly men, would be murdered outright or sent to detention camps to die. The Serb-run camps were as primitive as animal pens, lacking sanitary facilities or even space in which to move around. The women, who had been sent off on their own, later reported that the majority had been subjected to rape, often resulting in unwanted pregnancies. Humiliation, physical atrocities, and mental cruelty were inflicted without restraint on the 100,000 Muslims who would eventually lose their lives and on the deeply damaged survivors.

The name given to this assault on innocent town and city dwellers, whose families had lived for generations in the Yugoslav republic of Bosnia-Herzegovina, was "ethnic cleansing." Who were their Serb oppressors, and why did this attempt to drive them from their homeland take place after decades of multiethnic peace within the small, landlocked republic in the Balkan nation of Yugoslavia?

The Serbs Embark on Ethnic Cleansing

The death of Tito, Yugoslavia's leader for three-and-a-half decades, left the six republics without a single political figure capable of heading the nation. Nor—in the waning days of world Communism—did the Communist doctrine that Tito had suc-cessfully employed continue to have the power to unite the country as it had in the past.

Marshal Josip Broz Tito, photographed on the cover of *Picture Post* in 1944 bathing his dog during a break in World War II fighting, led Yugoslavia for about thirty-five years. On his death, the federation he had built fell apart.

A Balkan Patchwork

Six countries—Albania, Bulgaria, Greece, parts of Romania and Turkey, and most of Yugoslavia—made up the Balkan Peninsula of southeastern Europe for most of the twentieth century. Early in the century the region became known as "the powder keg of Europe" because so many wars, including World War I, sprang from its fierce and combative peoples, who were politically manipulated by the powerful kingdoms of the day.

The nation of Yugoslavia ("land of the South Slavs") was a patchwork of ethnicities, languages, and religions. It consisted of Slavic peoples, originally from Poland and Russia, such as Serbs, Croats, and Slovenes, as well as Turks and Albanians. Serbs followed the Eastern Orthodox Christian religion and wrote their version of the Serbo-Croatian language in the Greek-derived Cyrillic alphabet, which is related to the Russian alphabet.

Croats and Slovenes followed the Roman Catholic religion and wrote Serbo-Croatian in the Latin alphabet. The descendants of the Turks who settled in the land of the South Slavs in the 1300s adopted Slavic culture to a degree but clung to Islam, as did the Albanians living to the south.

The two world wars politically united the diverse peoples of Yugoslavia, the first war into the Kingdom of Serbs, Croats, and Slovenes, and the second war into a federal republic made up of six autonomous republics and two autonomous provinces. Serbia, political center of the onetime kingdom, held sway over the others and contained the national capital, Belgrade.

But the other independent republics—Bosnia, Croatia, Slovenia, Montenegro, and Macedonia—had their own capitals, presidents, and legislative bodies. Under the slogan "Brotherhood and Unity," wartime resistance leader and Communist strongman Josip Broz, better known as Tito, held the new Yugoslavia together from 1945 until his death in 1980. His death was followed by questions about which of the presidents of the six republics would take over and how the patchwork of Yugoslavia's peoples would fare now that the fabled and charismatic Tito was gone.

After 1980 a rotating presidency was tried but proved unsuccessful. It appeared inevitable that the president of one of the six federated republics would eventually try to step into the leadership position formerly occupied by Tito. And this was the case. In 1991 Slobodan Milosevic, president of Serbia since 1989, made a move toward Serb nationalism—the extension of Serb power into all the other republics in which Serbs lived.

How could such a program be carried out in a nation where almost every republic had only a Serb minority—one that intermingled and even intermarried with non-Serbs? Croatia was inhabited principally by Roman Catholic Croats, although its border areas especially were comprised of more than 35 percent Eastern Orthodox Serbs. Bosnia was a republic that was mainly Muslim. But Croats and Serbs lived there, too. Similar multiethnic groups comprised the other autonomous republics and provinces.

For generations people of many ethnic backgrounds and several different religions, dwelling side by side, had enjoyed peaceful living conditions. Milosevic sought to disrupt this amity. To create a greater Serbia, Milosevic was prepared to cleanse the other republics of all but their Serb populations, even though Serbs were in the minority within them.

Wary of Serbia's encroaching nationalism, the republics of Slovenia, Croatia, and Bosnia made plans to secede, or disassociate, from the federated nation of Yugoslavia. Slovenia, in northwestern Yugoslavia, was a semi-alpine republic bordering Austria that was more culturally allied to western Europe. Its Slovene language, although related to Serbo-Croatian, was written in the Latin alphabet. Many Slovenians also spoke German, and most were Roman Catholic.

As the most prosperous of the six republics, Slovenia had long resented its mandated contributions to the economic development of the poorer republics, such as Muslim Macedonia, which was originally settled by Turks and then inhabited by Greeks and Bulgarians.

On June 25, 1991, Slovenia's president announced the independence of his republic, no longer to be affiliated with Yugoslavia. Milosevic, hardly ready to accept such an affront to the Serb nation that he was envisaging, dispatched the Yugoslav Peoples' Army to Slovenia. What followed was a minor war, lasting only ten days and with only forty-four military and a handful of civilian deaths. And, by July 8, Milosevic and Slovenia's president Milan Kucan had come to terms.

Milosevic's change of heart regarding Slovenia's independence had come about quickly. Why put his power grab at risk for a small republic that counted almost no Serbs among its population? Threats of secession by other republics with large Serb populations would be met, however, with severe measures. Already, in fact, Croatia's president, Franjo Tudjman, had declared independence for his republic, also on June 25, 1991.

In August 1991, full-scale war broke out between Croatia and Serbia, and ethnic cleansing began in earnest. This effort to remove Croats from their own villages and to give their holdings to their Serb neighbors was enforced not just by the Yugoslav Peoples' Army but also by Serb paramilitaries, under the command of an army lieutenant colonel named Ratko Mladic. Brutal treatment of Croat civilians followed. They were robbed of their property, raped and beaten, and confined to overcrowded prison cells.

November 1991 saw the fall of the town of Vukovar, on Croatia's eastern border with Serbia. Although Vukovar's population was 43.7 percent Croat and 37.4 percent Serb, the Serbs claimed it for their own. After it had been under siege by the Serbs for three months, whose aim was to evacuate or kill its Croat residents, "Corpses of people and animals littered the streets. Grisly skeletons of buildings still burned, barely a square inch had escaped damage. Serbian volunteers, wild-eyed, roared down the streets, their pockets full of looted treasures." By the end of 1991 an embattled Croatia had won its independence. But it had lost nearly half its territory to

Serbia, and much of it was under occupation by the enemy.

Bosnia-Herzegovina, most often referred to as Bosnia, was the next republic to attempt secession in the face of Milosevic's effort to dismantle Yugoslavia and create a greater Serbia on its former territory. Bosnia's declaration of independence took place in March 1992 and was recognized by both the United States and the European Community. Alija Izetbegovic, a Muslim, had been president of Bosnia since 1990, as a result of multiparty elections. He represented not only Bosnia's largest ethnic group—its 44-percent Muslim population—but also its lesser percentages of Serbs (32 percent) and Croats (19 percent).

Despite the Serb minority in Bosnia, a new "Bosnian Serb" leader, Radovan Karadzic, took charge of the political and military assault. Among the first strikes was a major attack on the Bosnian capital of Sarajevo, a city dominated by mosques and minarets, but one in which Muslims, Serbs, and Croats had lived together for five hundred years. Set among steep hills, Sarajevo had also been the site of the 1984 Winter Olympics.

On April 5, 1992, as thousands of unarmed Sarajevo citizens of all faiths and nationalities marched through the city protesting ethnic divisions and proclaiming tolerance, the first shots from Serb artillery rang out. This was the beginning of the siege of Sarajevo, which would last for nearly four years, until officially declared ended early in 1996.

During that time Sarajevo would become crowded with refugees from the surrounding towns and villages that had been overtaken by the Serbs. The Bosnian Serbs blockaded the roads and shut down the airport, preventing the besieged city from receiving food, water, medicine, and other vital supplies, and frequently shelling its 400,000 residents from the surrounding heights. Sniper attacks were common.

Air assaults, too, took place at the hands of a now well-organized Serb military force of 80,000 under the command of Major

A soldier and civilians come under fire from Serbian snipers in downtown Sarajevo.

General (soon to be Lieutenant General) Ratko Mladic, working along-side political leader Radovan Karadzic. Cease-fires brokered by western nations were constantly violated, and the violations went unpunished. Nor did the European powers and the United States provide more than humanitarian aid in the form of air drops and relief convoys, the latter arranged by the United Nations with the grudging permission of the Bosnian Serbs.

Not until August 1995, when the western powers of the North Atlantic Treaty Organization (NATO) finally voted to bomb the Bosnian Serb positions around Sarajevo, did the Serbs begin to loosen their grip on the battered city. By the time the siege ended, 12,000 civilians had been killed in Sarajevo and more than 50,000 had been wounded.

During that period the Serbs vigorously pursued their policy of ethnic cleansing in Bosnia's other towns and villages. On August 14, 1992, U.S. diplomat Richard Holbrooke witnessed a scene in the small city of Banja Luka in northern Bosnia, where "at close to gunpoint, Muslims are signing papers giving up their personal property, either to neighbors or in exchange for the right to leave Bosnia. Then they are herded onto buses headed for the border. . . . Some leave quietly, others crying. This is the end of their lives in an area their families have lived in for centuries."

Many of the Muslim refugees never reached the border. Their lives ended in detention camps reminiscent of the Nazi death camps of World War II. As reported by journalist Roy Gutman of the New York newspaper *Newsday*, "Heads bowed and hands clasped behind their backs, the Muslim prisoners lined up before their Serb captors. One by one they sat on the metal stool and then knelt to have their heads shaved." Those who did not die of starvation and disease in the Serb camps became victims of either random or selective killings, preceded by orders to dig their own graves.

The Story of Srebrenica, a Bosnian "Safe Area"

East of Sarajevo, close to the border with Serbia, lies the city of Srebrenica, named for the silver mining that once took place in the vicinity (*srebren* is the Serbo-Croatian word for silver). The city's population of 37,000 was 75 percent Muslim and 25 percent Serb. Early in the conflict between Serbia and Bosnia, it had been defended with some success.

In April 1993, however, as Serb advances against this part of Bosnia became more intense, the United Nations took action, declaring Srebrenica and five other towns and cities in the region to be "safe areas." A UN Protection Force (UNPROFOR) would police the "safe areas" to oversee a hoped-for cessation of fighting in the battle between the Bosnian defenders and the increasingly threatening Bosnian Serbs, as well as to facilitate the entry of humanitarian aid and relief supplies to the besieged cities.

Lightly armed and backed with no more authority than the blue flag of the United Nations, the 7,400 troops contributed

The Death Camps of Bosnia and the International Community

Unlike genocides that took place behind a wall of silence, as did the one in Cambodia, the massacres in Bosnia were known to the outside world as early as May 1992, two months after President Izetbegovic had declared independence from the Federated Republic of Yugoslavia.

From within Bosnia came reports by eyewitnesses who had been present at the earliest ethnic cleansing procedures. The reports reached UN Secretary General Boutros Boutros-Ghali directly through Bosnia's ambassador to the United Nations. Journalists, aid workers, and even interested travelers came upon scenes in Bosnia of people being forcibly ejected from their homes, rounded up, beaten, jeered at and threatened, and roughly evacuated in buses or cattle cars.

By August 1992 crowding and starvation in the camps had reached such an intense degree that a writer for the *Guardian*, a British newspaper, attested to the following: "The men are at various stages of human decay and affliction; the bones of their elbows and wrists protrude like pieces of jagged stone from the pencil thin stalks to which their arms have been reduced." In addition to the written word, television transmitted scenes of horror that required no words to the outside world.

Although the United Nations, the European Community,

and the United States had been receiving timely reports of the atrocities committed in Bosnia, no action other than weak UN "peacekeeper" support was offered. The UN Security Council refused to lift the arms embargo placed on Bosnia at the start of the conflict (even though its antagonist, Serbia, had boldly violated the order). And, by the end of 1992, "almost two million Bosnians—nearly half the population—had lost their homes."

In a January 1993 memorandum from U.S. diplomat Richard Holbrooke to the incoming administration of President Bill Clinton, the following observations and recommendations were made. Holbrooke, who had in an unofficial capacity been witness to the scene in Bosnia during the past year, noted that due to the arms embargo, the Bosnian government had been turning to the Islamic nations of the Middle East, including Iran, for weapons. He therefore urged that the UN embargo be lifted at the behest of the United States.

Holbrooke also suggested that the United States brand such Bosnian Serb leaders as Radovan Karadzic and Ratko Mladic war criminals to be harshly dealt with by the international community after the conflict ended. He further advised that in order "to save as many lives as possible in Bosnia . . . to make containment of the war a top priority . . . to punish the Serbs for their behavior" the United States should "in concert with other nations" create "some sort of ad hoc military coalition."

Holbrooke did not feel that the international community should get involved in a ground war in the region. But he did favor "Direct use of force against the Serbs: Bombing the Bosnian Serbs and even Serbia proper if necessary." Holbrooke's memorandum received no reply when it was received in Washington shortly after Clinton's inauguration, nor did other nations respond to his suggestion. The genocide in Bosnia would continue.

by member nations were hardly in a position to maintain disarmament. As in the cases of Cambodia, Rwanda, and Darfur, the United Nations was to prove weak in preventing crimes against humanity and ineffective in punishing them. The Bosnian Serbs had already knocked out the water supplies, electricity, and other basic services in the region. And, as they gained ground in the rest of Bosnia through ethnic cleansing followed by mass murder, they tightened the noose around the eastern enclaves, bursting with a bottled-up population of Muslim refugees.

The UNPROFOR assignment limped along for two years until, on July 6, 1995, General Ratko Mladic unleashed his frustrations on the "safe area" of Srebrenica. In a week that began with the shelling of what proved to be the most unsafe city in the world, the Bosnian Serbs carried out, in the words of Richard Holbrooke, "the biggest single mass murder in Europe since World War II."

Upon entering the city, Mladic's forces rounded up men and boys in the thousands, shooting them on the spot, herding them into the soccer stadium to be executed, or shoving them onto buses to be taken to adjacent killing sites. The Dutch UNPROFOR peacekeepers, of which there were 370, were taken hostage. Controversy persists to this day as to whether the Dutch protectors had been lax in their duty and had even fraternized with the Serb forces. But their number appears too small to have been effective either way. In all, some eight thousand Muslim men and boys between the ages of twelve and sixty were murdered in the fall of Srebrenica. Untold numbers of women and girls were raped.

The futility of UNPROFOR's position in Bosnia was clearly demonstrated. "The Dutch peace-keepers stationed there did not know what to do. [On July 7] a peace-keeper retreating with his unit after Serb forces had overrun their observation post had his head blown off—hit not by Serbs but by Bosnian government soldiers who had wanted to stop the retreat of the Dutch troops from government front-line positions."

Pleas from the Dutch commander at Srebrenica for air strikes against the Serbs were denied as being too "dangerous," despite past humiliations of UNPROFOR troops. At other "safe areas" the Serbs had "handcuffed [French soldiers] to trees and telephone poles. The world's press was invited to film these men standing miserably in the broiling sun . . . waving white flags of surrender, to the horror of the new French President, Jacques Chirac."

When would the American, French, British, and other members of NATO finally take action against the slaughter that had made the United Nations' efforts at controlling it a mockery? Since taking office in 1993, President Clinton had remained indecisive regarding involvement in Bosnia, fearful of being drawn into a stalemate or, as the Bosnian Serb leader Radovan Karadzic threateningly termed it, "another Vietnam." Srebrenica, however, with its ruthless civilian killings and its massive death pits, left little choice for Clinton but to intervene.

On August 30, 1995, a coordinated NATO bombing by more than sixty aircraft flying from an American aircraft carrier and from bases in Italy pounded Bosnian Serb positions around the still-besieged city of Sarajevo. The massive air strikes of Operation Deliberate Force, as the mission was named, continued into September of 1995 and took out strategic Serb emplacements in and around the other "safe areas" that had been under siege.

The NATO bombings of August 1995 finally crippled the efforts of Milosevic and his chief henchmen in Bosnia, Karadzic and Mladic, to continue the genocide of the Bosnian Muslims. But it was too late for the 100,000 victims of the Serbs' ethnic cleansing campaign, who now lay nameless—most of them intentionally stripped of their identities before execution—in mass graves.

At last, a draft for a peace agreement was reached, with Richard Holbrooke of the United States as chief negotiator between the western powers and the presidents of the three former Yugoslav republics—Milosevic of Serbia, Izetbegovic of Bosnia, and

Tudjman of Croatia. The terms of the peace agreement were worked out between November 1 and November 21 at Wright-Patterson Air Force Base in Dayton, Ohio. In attendance were the three Yugoslav presidents along with staff members as well as high-ranking American political and military officials.

The presidents of Bosnia and Croatia, the two republics that had been attacked by the Serbs and suffered the effects of ethnic cleansing, were understandably hostile toward Milosevic, the Serb president. There was also distrust between them. Personalities clashed, and difficulties were encountered at every turn. Human rights, the punishment of war criminals, and the future ethnic composition of Bosnia were of special concern. Nearly 2 million Bosnian Muslims had been displaced, including 300,000 who had fled to Germany. Where in Bosnia would they relocate, and should a portion of Bosnia be assigned to its onetime Bosnian Serb population?

In what has come to be seen by many analysts as an unsatisfactory and even perilous solution, the territory formerly known as Bosnia was divided into two approximately equal-size entities. The newly named Bosnian Federation was to consist of a majority of Bosnian Muslims (53 percent) followed by a lesser number (41 percent) of Bosnian Croats. The other half of the former Bosnia was to be known as Republika Srpska and would be occupied by Bosnian Serbs, who would make up nearly 90 percent of its population.

To give the Serbs roughly half of a country in which they had originally comprised only 32 percent of the entire population seemed unjust to many analysts who had not participated in the Dayton negotiations. Perils for the future existed, too. The Bosnian Federation might decide to lay claim to all of its former territory; the Republika Srpska might wish to join with Serbia proper.

Nonetheless, the Dayton Agreement was signed in Paris on December 14, 1995, by the Americans, including President Bill Clinton, as well as the leaders of France, the United Kingdom,

Germany, and Russia. To monitor and implement its terms, militarily if necessary, a NATO-led Implementation Force (IFOR) was deployed. As the representative of the nations that brought an end to Serb aggression in the former republics of Croatia and Bosnia, IFOR proved more effective in maintaining and enforcing peace than had UNPROFOR.

The Fate of the Serb War Criminals

In the words of Richard Holbrooke, on November 22, 1995, "the arrest of Karadzic and Mladic was the most critical issue that was not resolved at Dayton. I repeated . . . that if the two men, particularly Karadzic, the founder and leader of a still-unrepentant separatist movement, remained at large, full implementation of the agreement would be impossible."

This graphic gives the details of the crimes for which Radovan Karadzic and Ratko Mladic were sought for trial by The Hague's international tribunal.

Holbrooke's use of the words "separatist movement" referred to a split that had taken place in June 1995 between Slobodan Milosevic, the president of Serbia, and his two Bosnian Serb brethren. As the war with Bosnia dragged on, Serbia and Serbs everywhere had come to be seen as ruthless aggressors. As a result, the republic of Serbia was suffering from economic woes and energy shortages and was isolated by trade sanctions imposed from abroad.

Although there was no question that the nationalist ambitions of Milosevic had ignited the conflict with Croatia and Bosnia, the Serb president now tried to gain respectability by softening his stance. Nor did he wish to be closely associated with the power-hungry Karadzic and Mladic who, in addition to their crimes against humanity, were said to be involved in war profiteering and money laundering.

Making his appearance at Dayton as president of Serbia, Milosevic was for the most part genial and surprisingly cooperative. Although claiming to have little influence with the warring parties on the Serb side, he made minor concessions that eased some of the tensions. He even referred to Karadzic and Mladic as "those idiots from Pale [the mountain capital of the Bosnian Serbs]" and cautioned against bringing them to any sort of international meeting, thus gaining a temporary measure of regard and trust for himself.

Having been successful in obtaining 49 percent of Bosnia for its Serb population—to be known as Republika Srpska—Milosevic left Dayton a respected negotiator and returned to Belgrade. But his ambition to expand his domain into a Greater Serbia had not died with the losses in Croatia and Bosnia. As early as 1987 Milosevic had seized on the idea of expanding Serbia by driving out the 90 percent Albanian population of the autonomous province of Kosovo in southern Yugoslavia, which shared part of its border with Albania.

Six hundred years earlier, in 1389, the Serbs had suffered a massive defeat by the Turks on the battlefield known as Kosovo Polje, and the area had subsequently become the home of Muslim peoples, especially Albanians. In 1989, when he became president of Serbia, Milosevic began to suppress the rights of the Muslim majority and to destroy the autonomy of the province, favoring its small Serb minority. Kosovo, in turn, began a movement for secession and independence.

In 1998, three years after Dayton, Milosevic was carrying out a campaign of ethnic cleansing against Kosovar Albanians. Outright murder and the creation of hundreds of thousands of refugees took place, as did fighting between the Kosovo Liberation Army (KLA) and the Serbian military and police.

Ultimatums from NATO to Milosevic to halt the genocide in Kosovo had no effect and, from March to June 1999, the western powers carried out their threat of air strikes against targets in Kosovo and Serbia. Operation Allied Force, as the strategic bombing campaign was called, knocked out major public services and vital commercial installations in the Serbian capital of Belgrade. The images of parts of a European city being shattered by air assaults were shocking indeed, but there appeared to be no other way of curbing the feverish nationalist onslaughts of the Serbian president.

Could Milosevic remain a power figure in Serbia following the eleven weeks of NATO bombing that he had invited *and* his forced withdrawal from Kosovo, from which 100,000 Serb inhabitants (nearly half the Kosovo Serb population) had been forced to flee? As public opinion turned against him, his grip on the presidency began to loosen. A new coalition of leaders pledging themselves to multi-ethnic peace rose to power and, following the disputed elections of 2000, Milosevic was forced to resign the presidency under accusations of wrongdoing and amid demonstrations calling for his punishment. On March 31, 2001, his own government arrested him on suspicion of corruption, abuse of power, and embezzlement.

But charges of crimes against humanity, violations of wartime behavior, breaches of the Geneva Conventions, and genocide in Croatia, Bosnia, and Kosovo were awaiting him at the International

An Albanian woman cries after looking at the damage to her home as a result of Serb attacks on Kosovo, Yugoslavia. The ethnic Albanian majority in Kosovo had resisted the Serbian forces led by Slobodan Milosevic.

Criminal Tribunal for the Former Yugoslavia (ICTY) in The Hague in the Netherlands. Milosevic was sent there early in 2002.

Obstinate to the last, the man who had fomented genocidal war in Europe insisted on conducting his own defense. During his time in the War Criminal Prison in The Hague, Milosevic suffered from a heart ailment, often insisting on medicating himself. His trial was still in progress after nearly five years when he died in his prison cell on March 11, 2006, apparently of a heart attack. Humanity was thus robbed of hearing the evidence that might have been brought forth by the court on the charge of genocide and of the outcome for the defendant.

The ICTY had been founded in 1993 for the specific purpose of dealing with the war crimes and crimes against humanity that had taken place in the former Yugoslavia since 1991. Slobodan Milosevic had been the first head of state to be indicted and brought to trial, but already scores of individuals—Bosnian Serb soldiers and their commanders, local police, and high government officials—had been indicted and many of them brought before the court.

The court's first conviction for genocide was that of Radislav Krstic, the general who was second in command to Ratko Mladic and had ordered the massacre of eight thousand men and boys in Srebrenica in July 1995. In August 2001 the fifty-three-year-old Krstic was sentenced to forty-six years in prison. Relatives of Srebrenica victims were dissatisfied with the sentence (the tribunal's maximum sentence is life imprisonment). "Let him go and come back to us," a Srebrenica woman exclaimed. "We will give him a verdict. For 10,000 of our sons, only 46 years! His people have ripped my son from my arms." The families of the victims were further incensed when, in 2004, Krstic's sentence was reduced on appeal to thirty-five years, on the grounds that he was not a principal perpetrator of the genocide. The court concluded that he was only aiding and abetting, as ordered by his superior officers.

As late as 2008 the indicted Mladic, who had disappeared in 2001, and Karadzic, who had vanished in 1996, had not been apprehended. But in July 2008 Radovan Karadzic, the Bosnian Serb political leader and one of the world's most wanted war criminals, was arrested after twelve years in hiding. In recent years the fugitive Karadzic had radically disguised his appearance and had been living openly in Belgrade as a practitioner of alternative medicine.

No longer the robust supreme commander dressed in army fatigues and flaunting a shock of thick graying hair, Karadzic was now thinner, dressed in black, wore a full bushy beard and spectacles, and smoothed his hair back into a ponytail. How long he had been moving freely in Belgrade circles, sitting in cafes, writing and publishing articles, and giving lectures under the name "Dr. Dabic" was not known. It appeared that some people who knew his true identity shielded him because they did not find his genocidal campaign to obliterate the Bosnian Muslims a crime against humanity.

It is believed that what finally convinced the Serb authorities to deliver the indicted Karadzic to the ICTY was Serbia's interest in allying itself with its former enemies in the West and its desire to one day be welcomed into the world's biggest trading bloc, the European Union.

The evildoing that took place in the former Yugoslavia between 1992 and 1999, with regard to Croatia, Bosnia, and Kosovo has often been blamed on longtime ethnic hatreds. But this is proved untrue by the centuries during which multiethnic groups successfully lived side by side and intermingled throughout the region. The true reason for the genocides that were committed rests with the country's power-seeking criminal demagogues, starting with Milosevic.

The tendency to blame every Serb for the slaughter in Bosnia and elsewhere is erroneous, too. Croats, Bosnians, and Kosovars also committed atrocities in defense of their ethnic integrity. But the fact remains that the Serb attempts at ethnic cleansing were at the root of the 100,000 Bosnian deaths and the numerous others that took place in Croatia and Kosovo.

There is no question that earlier action on the part of the West would have curbed the onslaught in Bosnia and saved hundreds of thousands of lives. But for too long a time the United States and the other members of NATO allowed a feeble and powerless UN contingent to serve as the sole protector of people against ruthless killers. What will it take for the West to react more quickly—or at all—to present and future genocides around the world? Or will Bosnia prove to have been a singular example, largely because of its location in Europe rather than in Africa or Asia?

5 Darfur and the Consequences of the Previous Genocides

A DECADE INTO THE TWENTY-FIRST CENTURY THE genocide in Darfur, which began in 2003, raged on amidst failed truce efforts. The drought-ridden landscape of western Sudan lay swept bare of its small subsistence-farming communities as a result of relentless attacks by the government of Sudan and its hired assassins, the Janjaweed. Where had the 2.5 million or more displaced villagers and small farmers of Darfur gone?

At least one million were crammed into internally displaced persons (IDP) camps in Darfur, while others had crossed the western border into the neighboring country of Chad. Maintenance of the IDP camps, some housing as many as 90,000 people, was wholly dependent on aid organizations such as the Red Cross, Doctors Without Borders, Oxfam, CARE, and humanitarian programs of the United Nations. Even with the ministrations of dedicated volunteers, the impoverished inhabitants of the camps were constantly threatened by water shortages, disease, and the ongoing fears of rape and murder by the marauding Janjaweed.

The same was true for those Darfuris driven from their homes who sought refuge in Chad, where at least twelve camps have been set up under the supervision of the UN High Commissioner for Refugees (UNHCR). Arriving on foot with only the possessions

An armed Sudanese rebel from the Justice and Equality Movement arrives at the abandoned village of Chero Kasi less than an hour after Janjaweed militia set it ablaze on September 7, 2004.

they could carry, the refugees told the all-too-familiar stories of having been bombed with explosives dropped from low-flying planes and then being massacred by the Janjaweed "devils on horseback."

As described by Jonathan Harr, reporting in the *New Yorker* on January 5, 2009, "The *janjaweed* killed those who had not fled into the bush, poisoned wells with their corpses, raped girls and women, set buildings ablaze, destroyed stocks of food and seed, trampled fields, and hacked down fruit trees."

Among the tens of thousands of displaced villagers who set

92

out for Chad, most were women and children, survivors of the killings aimed largely at men. Their place of refuge, however, presented numerous problems. Chad was a much poorer country than Sudan, ranking fifth from the bottom in a UN index of human development. Water, sewage systems, and electricity were in extremely short supply, a civil war was taking place under the rule of a corrupt president, and "The *janjaweed* were making raids across the border, stealing cattle and killing people."

Before the first camps were opened in 2004, the refugees sheltered, as in the Darfur camps, under rags suspended from sticks thrust into the ground. Wells were scarce, and the desert terrain provided water only in holes dug into the dry riverbeds. Once the Chadian camps were opened along the 400-mile border with Darfur, their populations quickly swelled.

The UNHCR cleared land, erected tents, and installed water and sewage systems. Gradually markets were established in the camps. The former Darfuri villagers traded homegrown vegetables and firewood for manufactured goods such as tools and cloth. Barbershops and tea shops sprang up, and some of the refugees even found jobs outside the camps. But the tent cities offered only a temporary solution at best. Would the refugees ever return to their own land and reestablish an independent means of survival?

The Unsolved Problem of the Genocide in Darfur

Despite the efforts of the UNHCR, escape to the already overcrowded camps in Chad was not the answer for the entire population of Darfur, originally numbering 6 to 7 million. And, while the international community may have pondered responses to the genocide in Darfur since it began in 2003, the only decisive step taken to seek redress for Sudan's victims was the indictment of its president, Omar al-Bashir, by the International Criminal Court (ICC) on March 4, 2009.

The ICC, founded in 2002 by a coalition of world nations at a treaty signing in Rome, is a permanent tribunal that generally meets in The Hague, the Netherlands. Its purpose has been to prosecute individuals responsible for genocide, crimes against humanity, and war crimes since the date of its founding. President al-Bashir was the first sitting head of state to be issued an arrest warrant by the court for "intentionally directing attacks against . . . the civilian population of Darfur, Sudan, murdering, exterminating, raping, torturing and forcibly transferring large numbers of civilians and pillaging their property."

Although the court did not extend the charges against the Sudanese president to that of genocide, al-Bashir reacted with anger and contempt, declaring that the warrant would "not be worth the ink it is written with" and that the tribunal could "eat" it. As the ICC has no police force or other means of delivering those charged with crimes to the court, it seemed doubtful that Omar al-Bashir would face trial.

The president referred to his accusers as colonialists who had been defeated before and would be defeated again and, in retaliation, he ordered thirteen aid groups to leave Sudan, including some divisions of Doctors Without Borders. Among those permitted to remain, three aid workers from a Belgian branch of the medical aid organization were kidnapped, apparently by bandits seeking ransom.

The expulsion of the aid groups was another blow for the victims of the Sudanese government's policies. Health care, water, and food are desperately needed by the Darfuris in the IDP camps. As Nicholas Kristof wrote in the *New York Times* on March 7, 2009, "The biggest immediate threat isn't starvation, because that takes time. Rather, the first crisis will be disease and water shortages, particularly in West Darfur.

"The camps will quickly run out of clean water, because generator-operated pumps bring the water to the surface from wells and boreholes. Fuel supplies to operate the pumps may last a couple of weeks, and then the water disappears. . . . Health clinics have already closed, and diarrhea is spreading . . . and meningitis. . . . Children will be the first to die."

The final words about the genocide in Darfur have not yet been written. As a war of extermination waged on a so-called racially different group, it constitutes the first major crime against humanity of the twenty-first century. Like the genocides of the twentieth century, it will be notorious principally for its cost in human life.

National or international tribunals may be created to examine the underlying causes and the nature of the aggression and to prosecute those found to be guilty. The latter may get off lightly or may receive harsh sentences. The massacre of 1.5 million Armenians in Ottoman Turkey resulted in hangings and jail sentences for relatively few of the perpetrators of the genocide (which did not then bear that name).

The murder of 6 million Jews in Nazi Germany was much more severely dealt with during the post–World War II Nuremberg Trials. But the question remains: In cases where the deliberate and systematic destruction of a people for reasons of race, ethnicity, nationality, or religion has taken place, and intervention is absent or inadequate, can justice ever be served?

Punishment for the Guilty After the UN Treaty on Genocide

During the war crimes trials directly following Turkey's attempt to exterminate the Armenians and the Nazis' efforts to wipe out the Jews of Europe, the word "genocide" was not part of the international vocabulary. Although the exiled Polish Jew Raphael Lemkin coined it in 1943, this crime against humanity was not officially documented until it was identified and defined by the UN Convention on the Prevention and Punishment of the Crime of Genocide (CPPCG) in 1948.

Aftermaths of the Armenian and Jewish Genocides

Denial by the Republic of Turkey of the Armenian massacre of 1915 to 1918 has continued into the twenty-first century. The organized killings of Armenians that occurred both before and after those dates are also denied. Turkish nationalists consider the topic taboo, and Turkish officials dispute any accusations that genocide took place.

When the well-known Turkish author Orhan Pamuk raised the topic in an interview with the Swiss publication *Das Magazin* in February 2005, he was forced to flee the country. "Thirty thousand Kurds have been killed here, and a million Armenians. And almost nobody dares to mention that. But I do," Pamuk declared. Later that year, on receiving a literary award in Germany, Pamuk repeated the charge against his government.

In December 2005 Pamuk returned to Turkey to face trial under a recently introduced law punishing anyone who insulted the Republic of Turkey with six months to three years in prison. The new law, however, had been passed *after* Pamuk's original remark, and he was given a partial reprieve, accused only of "insulting Turkishness." The following year Pamuk received the 2006 Nobel Prize in Literature, the first Turkish citizen ever to have been awarded the prestigious international prize.

Comparatively little has been written about the Armenians who survived the massacre that took place in World War I

Turkey. After 1918 some 10 million Armenian people scattered to other parts of the world, including France, Argentina, and the United States. Others moved to the small independent country of Armenia, which, as part of a postwar international treaty, was carved out of a border area between Turkey and Russia.

In 1920 the tiny nation, about the size of Maryland, was absorbed into the Soviet Union as a result of the Bolshevik Revolution. It did not regain its independence until September 21, 1991, when the Soviet Union dissolved. Today the Republic of Armenia, with a population of about 3 million, is struggling to make progress economically. In a historic agreement that took place in 2009, Turkey and Armenia established diplomatic relations for the first time.

At the beginning of World War II, Adolf Hitler made the self-assured remark that no one "today, after all, speaks of the annihilation of the Armenians." His belief that this, among other

Nobel Prize winner Orhan Pamuk spoke in front of the house of Hrant Dink, an Armenian-Turkish journalist who was assassinated as he left his newspaper office in 2007.

reasons, gave him license to kill 6 million Jews and an additional 5 million European civilians resulted in the postwar Nuremberg Trials, which took place in the German city of that name in 1945 and 1946.

No permanent international court of criminal justice existed at the time, so the trials were held at the behest of the United States, Great Britain, France, and the Soviet Union. At the first Nuremberg Trial, the prosecuting nations indicted twenty-four and tried twenty-one of Nazi Germany's major war criminals from among its political, military, and economic leaders. Of those found guilty, a number received death sentences or, alternately, life imprisonment. The second set of Nuremberg Trials dealt with lesser war criminals, including judges and doctors.

Unlike any nation before or since that has been charged with crimes against humanity, postwar Germany has engaged in a program of making reparations both to world Jewry and to the state of Israel, totaling more than $35 billion so far. Speaking in the Bundestag (German national parliament) on September 27, 1951, the West German chancellor Konrad Adenauer made the following declaration: "The Federal government and the great majority of the German people are deeply aware of the im-measurable suffering endured by the Jews of Germany and by the Jews of the occupied territories during the period of National Socialism [Nazism]. . . . In our name, unspeakable crimes have been committed and they demand restitution, both moral and material, for the persons and properties of the Jews who have been so seriously harmed. . . ."

In 1938, just before the outbreak of World War II, the Jewish population of the world was 16.5 million. Today, even after postwar recovery, it measures 13.2 million, with a growth rate close to zero.

By 1951 the required number of twenty UN member states had ratified the CPPCG, and the treaty went into effect. Of the five permanent members of the UN Security Council, only France was among the original twenty signers. The Soviet Union ratified the CPPCG in 1954, the United Kingdom in 1970, and the People's Republic of China in 1983. The United States (the fifth member of the Security Council) did not ratify the treaty until 1988. Among world nations to sign on to the CPPCG, today numbering more than 140, the United States was ninety-eighth.

Why did it take forty years for the United States, a nation founded on guarantees of human rights and freedoms and multi-cultural in its composition, to ratify the treaty condemning the crime that Lemkin named as early as 1943?

Although President Harry Truman had called for ratification in June 1949, both Congress and Truman's successors, starting with Dwight D. Eisenhower, looked to the international treaty as a source of possible threats *against* the United States. Was the United States entirely free of genocidal guilt? There were so many ethnic, racial, religious, and cultural groups, past or present, who might bring charges.

Potential accusations ranged from the persecution and mass killing of American Indians beginning in the late fifteenth century to contemporary mob assaults on such minorities as homosexuals, African Americans, Jews, and many immigrants. The treaty permitted the intervention of foreign powers in a sovereign nation in which a form of genocide was perceived to be taking place. Suppose that sovereign nation turned out to be the United States.

Almost single-handedly Senator William Proxmire of Wisconsin took up the cause of the ratification of the CPPCG. For nineteen years, from 1967 to 1986, he gave almost daily speeches before Congress—3,211 in all—urging acceptance of the treaty. Only a tactical blunder on the part of President Ronald Reagan, in 1985, appeared to have aroused such strong support for signing that Congress could no longer hold out against the CPPCG.

To commemorate the fortieth anniversary of the ending of World War II, President Reagan went to Germany in May 1985 to lay a wreath on a cemetery for German military war dead. No arrangement had been made, however, for him to visit a Holocaust site in remembrance of the war's Jewish victims. Popular outrage ensued.

The American president's excuse that he was trying to cement relations with Germany because German soldiers had also been victims of Nazism served only to heighten the fury of those who supported the acceptance of the CPPCG. To appease his critics, Reagan then tacked on a visit to the Bergen-Belsen concentration camp memorial.

Congress ratified the treaty on genocide in 1986. On signing it into law in 1988, President Reagan declared, "We finally close the circle today. I am delighted to fulfill the promise made by Harry Truman to all the peoples of the world and especially to the Jewish people."

But what, if any, immediate effect did the passage of the law to punish genocide have on U.S. policy in 1988? Since 1980 the nations of Iran and Iraq had been at war, and the United States had been supporting Iraq (partly in response to the Iranian hostage-taking of American citizens in 1979). Yet Iraq's president, Saddam Hussein, had long been persecuting the stateless Kurdish people who lived within his country's borders and who made up less than a quarter of its total population.

In 1987 and 1988 the Iraqi president stepped up his campaign to annihilate the Kurds, using poison gas and other chemical attacks, destroying villages, herding Kurds into killing sites, and burying them in mass graves. Hussein's excuse for the genocide of tens of thousands of Kurds was that they had been disloyal to Iraq, some disrupting the Iraqi war effort and others joining forces with the Iranian enemy. Yet relatively few of the targeted Kurds were soldiers, and the mass assaults were carried out indiscriminately against the civilian population.

Throughout Reagan's presidency, which ended in 1989, the United States continued to aid Iraq with agricultural and industrial-supply credits and appeared to accept the rationale of its oil-rich trading partner that attacks on the Kurds were justified. Fourteen years and three presidencies later, however, friendly relations with Saddam Hussein had been all but forgotten, and the Iraqi president was labeled an archenemy of the United States. In 2003 the administration of President George W. Bush presented to Congress its reasons for wanting to invade Iraq. Congress voted for the invasion, leading to a lengthy war that resulted in more than four thousand American casualties. It was soon learned, however, that the president and his vice president, Richard B. Cheney, had lied to Congress and the American people about Iraq's danger to the United States. On the basis of having caused hundreds of thousands of Iraqi deaths alone, might not the two leaders be considered war criminals?

How much does a nation's self-interest at a given time have to do with its willingness to take up the cause of a people targeted for genocide within another nation? Apparently, a great deal depends on the advantages to be gained or lost by moving against a government that is ruthlessly ridding itself of an unwanted minority.

The U.S. bombing of Cambodia as part of its war with Vietnam actually paved the way for the rise of the Khmer Rouge. Yet the United States never perceived itself as having been in any way responsible for the atrocities committed by Pol Pot's regime between 1975 and 1979, nor did it ever intervene to put a halt to them.

The 1994 slayings in Rwanda took place *after* the United States had ratified the CPPCG. The failure of the United States to reach a conclusion as to whether the massacre of 800,000 Tutsis and Hutu moderates was "genocide" or merely "acts of genocide" appeared to be little more than a means of exempting itself from its responsibility under the treaty. Can there really be any difference between mur-dering a people by means of a massive government campaign of extermination and a widely distributed chain of government-sanctioned killing squads? The apology of President Bill Clinton in 1998 was moving, but it did not bring back a single life.

The Failure of the United States to Stop Genocide: Justified or Not?

"We, the international community, should have been more active in the early stages of the atrocities in Rwanda in 1994, and called them what they were—genocide." These were the words of Madeleine Albright, secretary of state during the Clinton administration, delivered in a speech to the Organization of African Unity in 1997. Such regrets and apologies, including those of President Clinton, were abundant following the Rwandan genocide, but they did not alter the death toll of 800,000.

The belated intervention of the United States and its NATO allies in Bosnia at the time of the fall of Srebrenica in July 1995 and the U.S.-sponsored Dayton Agreement, which took place in December of that year, halted the Serb aggression and helped to stabilize the region. But 100,000 Bosnian deaths and the devastation visited on the surviving population could not be undone.

One of the reasons often cited by American officialdom for the failure to take action during the Rwandan genocide was the involvement of the United States, between 1992 and 1994, in the northeastern African country of Somalia. In 1992, during the administration of President George H. W. Bush, the U.S. Army undertook a humanitarian mission in the desertlike nation that borders the Indian Ocean.

The purpose of Operation Restore Hope, as the mission was known, was to put an end to starvation in Somalia's hinterlands, where farmers could not grow crops due to ongoing clan fighting

After the Cambodian and Rwandan Genocides

Although some of the 2 million killings in Cambodia can be attributed to variations in class, culture, and economic status rather than strictly to religious, racial, or ethnic differences, there is no question that one of the aims of the Khmer Rouge was to wipe out the Cham Muslims.

Their Muslim faith, manner of dress, family life, marriage, and other customs resulted in the extermination of a disproportionate number of Chams, perhaps as many as 500,000. Buddhism and Catholicism were other religions practiced in Cambodia that were wiped out by violent means. So at least a third of the 2 million Cambodian crimes against humanity were clearly definable as genocide.

Nearly twenty years were to pass, following the ousting of the Khmer Rouge by Vietnamese occupiers in 1979, until the 1997 request by the Cambodian government for a UN–backed war criminal court to try the surviving leaders of the Khmer Rouge regime. Another ten years passed before judges were sworn in and the names of five officials were presented to them.

In 2010 the trials were still under way. A major figure was the commandant of the notorious Tuol Sleng Torture Center, in which at least 16,000 prisoners accused of disloyalty were tortured until they were murdered or allowed to die. The sixty-six-year-old prison master, who was not detected and arrested until 1999, is known as Duch (pronounced DOIK), although his real name is Kaing Guek Eav.

Duch's defense, like that of lesser figures brought to trial for hideous crimes, was that he had no choice. Had he been unwilling to carry out the murders of the Tuol Sleng prisoners, he himself would have been killed.

Another Cambodian war criminal whose trial is scheduled for the near future is political leader Nuon Chea, second in command to the deceased Pol Pot. Repeated delays in the Cambodian government's prosecution of Nuon Chea make one wonder if the aged Khmer Rouge leader will

Former Khmer Rouge S-21 prison chief Kaing Guek Eav, known as Duch (center), stands in the courtroom at the Extraordinary Chambers Cambodia in Phnom Penh on December 5, 2008, where he was being tried for genocide.

survive to answer to the charges against him. Millions of Cambodians born after the Khmer Rouge's fall in 1979 have little or no awareness of that murderous regime. But educational groups are today sponsoring memorial visits to the killing fields and distributing a government-approved text to schoolchildren that reveals the horrors of the past in Nazi Germany and Rwanda, as well as in Cambodia.

In Rwanda, unlike Cambodia, it did not take as long as thirty years for the principal genocidal killers to be brought to trial. At the end of 1994, the year of the genocide, the UN Security Council established the International Criminal Tribunal for Rwanda (ICTR), which met in Arusha, Tanzania.

Hutu leaders finally brought to trial in 2002 included Colonel Théoneste Bagosora, who had fled to Cameroon, where he was apprehended. After five years of hearings during which Bagosora maintained his innocence, he was sentenced, in December 2008, to life in prison. The sixty-seven-year-old former army colonel was convicted of genocide, murder, extermination, rape, persecution, other inhumane acts, violence, and outrages upon personal dignity.

Specifically, the court determined that Bagosora bore ultimate responsibility for the sexual assault and murder of the Hutu moderate prime minister of Rwanda, Agathe Uwilingiyimana, for the deaths of the ten Belgian peacekeepers, and of four government opposition leaders in the beginning hours of the genocide, among his other crimes. A death sentence for Bagosora was not an option under the rules of the ICTR.

Within Rwanda hundreds of thousands of genocide suspects have been tried in what are known as Gacaca courts. Gacaca, which translates to "on the grass," is the word for Rwanda's traditional court system in which locally elected judges preside. Formerly, the function of these hearings, which literally take place outdoors at shady roadside sites, was to resolve everyday disputes within the community.

Since the genocide, the Gacaca courts have led the effort to unify and reconcile Rwanda's torn population by bringing those who committed genocidal acts against their neighbors to justice, largely through mandated community service. The guilty have been put to work building homes, planting crops and trees, and building roads to restore the infrastructure of the country as well as the destroyed property of the victims.

But the effects of the Hutu-on-Tutsi violence of 1994 are still evident in Rwanda. Many survivors on both sides of the conflict are impoverished, suffer from health problems including AIDS, and live with animosity toward their neighbors and the fear of violence. The genocide in Rwanda has also had serious effects on surrounding countries, especially the former Zaire (now the Democratic Republic of the Congo), where refugee Hutu militias have been pursued by Rwandan army troops. In Rwanda itself, peace seems to have taken hold. But whether true healing has occurred is yet to be seen.

among Somali warlords. No able central government existed in this failed state.

American efforts to airlift food and other relief supplies from Kenya into Somalia soon met with disaster. Lawless gangs seized the supplies, civil wars escalated, and chaos and anarchy reigned throughout the country. Inevitably, American troops became embroiled as they tried to provide a secure background for humanitarian assistance.

October 1993 saw the climactic events that led to the U.S. withdrawal from Somalia under President Bill Clinton, who had taken office in January of that year. In the battle of Mogadishu, named for the Somali capital, two American Black Hawk helicopters were downed, eighteen U.S. soldiers were killed by Somali mobs, and their bodies were dragged through the streets to the jeering of Somali civilians and the forces of the Somali warlord Mohamed Farah Aideed. Was the failed American military intervention in Somalia a justifiable excuse for denying adequate troop strength to UNAMIR in Rwanda and for Senator Bob Dole's statement of April 1994?

The United States has failed to stop genocide for a number of other reasons as well. At the time of the Armenian massacre, despite the detailed and harrowing reports sent to Washington by Ambassador Henry Morgenthau Sr., President Woodrow Wilson chose not to declare war on Turkey. He opted for the protection of American interests in the enemy nation and even appeared to accept the Turkish government's claim that the assault on the Armenians was a legitimate response to their disloyalty during World War I.

The failure to help the 6 million Jews of Europe who died under the Nazi regime may indeed have been caused by disbelief, the inability to accept that evil of such magnitude could exist. Recall the response of Supreme Court Justice Felix Frankfurter when Polish emissary Jan Karski presented him with proof of the existence of the death camps. Frankfurter, himself a Jew, seemed to

Evariste Mulangaria (right), accused of complicity in Rwanda's 1994 genocide, wipes his brow while under guard prior to his court appearance.

have been astonished by the longtime and widespread ordeals of his fellow religionists.

Yet other reasons for inaction abound. Officials voice the excuse that emotional factors are too likely to draw the nation into dangerous situations; that U.S. intervention may only increase the bloodshed; and that it is difficult to be sure the conflict at hand can be defined as genocide.

Is military action, such as the NATO bombing of the Bosnian Serb army emplacements above Sarajevo in 1995 and of the Serb capital of Belgrade in 1999 (to end the genocide in Kosovo) always necessary? Wouldn't an earlier response to Sarajevo and Kosovo have saved many lives and made for less violence and destruction in the long run?

Isn't it true that the United States and other members of the international community have many alternate resources if they truly wish to abide by their pledge to prevent and punish genocide around the world? Perpetrators can be expelled from the United Nations, their embassies abroad can be closed, foreign assets can be frozen, and economic sanctions can be applied. Genocidal authorities can be threatened with prosecution in international courts. And well-armed and effective peacekeeping forces can be provided through the United Nations. At the same time refugees from genocide can be housed in safe shelters that are capable of sustaining health and life.

Last, if American and worldwide attention to the crime of genocide is purely a matter of self-interest, what should that interest be? Can we, with a clear conscience, continue to live in a world where great numbers of innocent people periodically must die for their skin color, their religion, their race, their culture—their heritage?

Notes

Introduction

p. 10: "They came with horses . . .": "Darfur: Too Many People Killed for No Reason," *Amnesty International*, February 2004.

pp. 11–12: "They have a right to propose . . .": Sudan's secretary of state for foreign affairs, quoted in *Al-Anbaa*, March 4, 2004.

p. 12: "a coordinated effort, not just random . . .": Colin Powell, quoted in "Powell Declares Killing in Darfur 'Genocide,'" *Online NewsHour*, September 9, 2004, www.pbs.org/newshour/updates/sudan_09-09-04.html (accessed September 11, 2008).

Chapter 1

p. 16: "Who today, after all . . .": Adolf Hitler, quoted in Peter Balakian, *The Burning Tigris*, New York: HarperCollins, 2003, 377.

p. 19: "The measure of arming the Kurds . . .": the British consul to the Ottoman Empire, quoted in Balakian, *The Burning Tigris*, 50.

p. 20: "men, women, and children . . . most barbarously . . .": American missionary and relief workers, quoted in Balakian, *The Burning Tigris*, 66.

p. 21: "Turkey belongs only to the . . .": Mehmet Talaat, quoted in Balakian, *The Burning Tigris*, 172.

p. 22: "had been transformed into road . . .": Henry Morgenthau Sr., *Ambassador Morgenthau's Story*, New York: Doubleday and Doran, 1918, 302.

p. 23: "In almost all cases, the procedure . . . .": Morgenthau, *Ambassador Morgenthau's Story*, 302–303.

p. 24: "Deportation of and excesses against . . .": Henry Morgenthau, quoted in National Archives, *State Department Record*, Record Group 59.867.4016/76.

p. 28: "This is to avenge the death . . .": Soghomon Tehlirian, quoted in Samantha Power, *"A Problem from Hell:" America and the Age of Genocide*, New York: HarperCollins Perennial, 2003, 1.

p. 31: "Men, fourteen to sixty years . . .": Jewish Labor Bund, quoted in Martin Gilbert, *Auschwitz and the Allies*, New York: Holt, Rinehart and Winston, 1981, 40.

p. 32: "crime of murdering the entire Jewish . . .": Szmul Zygielbojm, quoted in "Pole's Suicide Note Pleads for Jews," the *New York Times*, June 4, 1943.

p. 32: "I don't believe you. . . .": Felix Frankfurter, quoted in Power, *"A Problem from Hell,"* 34.

p. 34: "Barbarity . . .": Raphael Lemkin, quoted in Power, *"A Problem from Hell,"* 21.

p. 36: "any of the following acts . . .": UN Convention on the Prevention and Punishment of the Crime of Genocide, quoted in Power, *"A Problem from Hell,"* 57.

Chapter 2

p. 39: "It was the morning of April 17, 1975 . . .": Moly Ly, quoted in Dith Pran, comp., and Kim DePaul, ed., *Children of Cambodia's Killing Fields: Memoirs by Survivors*, New Haven: Yale University Press, 1997, 57.

p. 39: "We walked with our bundles . . .": Ly, quoted in Pran, *Children of Cambodia's Killing Fields*, 58–59.

p. 42: "Soldiers drank water from toilet bowls . . .": Philip Short, *Pol Pot: Anatomy of a Nightmare*, New York: Henry Holt, 2004, 269.

p. 42: "It was a stupefying sight . . .": Short, *Pol Pot*, 272.

p. 45: "organisationally and . . .": Pol Pot, quoted in Short, *Pol Pot*, 170.

p. 45: "the great, guiding star . . .": Pol Pot, quoted in Short, *Pol Pot*, 170.

p. 48: "Along the roadside . . .": Short, *Pol Pot*, 310.

p. 48: "[It] bowled me over . . .": Prince Sihanouk, quoted in Short, *Pol Pot*, 333.

p. 53: "There were no food-stalls . . .": Elizabeth Becker, quoted in Samantha Power, *"A Problem from Hell:" America and the Age of Genocide*, New York: HarperCollins Perennial, 2003, 138.

p. 55: "the most serious that had occurred . . .": Becker, quoted in Power, *"A Problem from Hell,"* 154.

Chapter 3

p. 57: "screwdrivers, hammers . . .": Samantha Power, *"A Problem from Hell:" America and the Age of Genocide*, New York: HarperCollins Perennial, 2003, 334.

p. 62: "found 150 people, dead mostly . . .": Brent Beardsley, quoted in Power, *"A Problem from Hell,"* 349.

p. 62: "there were children . . .": Beardsley, quoted in Power, *"A Problem from Hell,"* 349.

p. 63: "I had accepted death. . . .": Laurent Nkongoli, quoted in Philip Gourevitch, *We Wish to Inform You That Tomorrow We Will Be Killed With Our Families: Stories from Rwanda*, New York: Farrar, Straus, 1998, 22.

p. 66: "You could literally see the blood . . .": Josh Hammer, quoted in Gourevitch, *We Wish to Inform You That Tomorrow We Will Be Killed With Our Families*, 117.

p. 66: "I don't think we have any national interest there. . . .": Bob Dole, quoted in Power, *"A Problem from Hell,"* 352.

p. 68: "Neither the United States . . .": Power, *"A Problem from Hell,"* 369.

p. 70: "We in the United States . . .": Bill Clinton, quoted in James Bennet, "Clinton Declares U.S., with World, Failed Rwandans," the *New York Times*, March 26, 1998.

Chapter 4

p. 71: "Two hundred Serb paramilitaries . . .": Laura Silber and Allan Little, *Yugoslavia: Death of a Nation*, New York: Penguin, 1996, 244.

p. 76: "Corpses of people and animals . . .": Silber and Little, *Yugoslavia*, 180.

pp. 78–79: "At close to gunpoint . . .": Richard Holbrooke, *To End a War*, New York: Random House, 1998, 37.

p. 79: "Heads bowed and hands clasped behind their backs . . .": Roy Gutman, quoted in Silber and Little, *Yugoslavia*, 249.

p. 80: "The men are at various stages . . .": Silber and Little, *Yugoslavia*, 250.

p. 81: "almost two million Bosnians . . .": Silber and Little, *Yugoslavia*, 252.

p. 81: "to save as many lives . . .": Holbrooke, *To End a War*, 51.

p. 81: "Direct use of force . . .": Holbrooke, *To End a War*, 52.

p. 82: "the biggest single mass murder . . .": Holbrooke, *To End a War*, 69.

p. 82: "The Dutch peace-keepers . . .": Silber and Little, *Yugoslavia*, 357.

p. 83: "handcuffed [French soldiers] to trees . . .": Holbrooke, *To End a War*, 64.

p. 85: "the arrest of Karadzic and Mladic . . .": Holbrooke, *To End a War*, 315.

p. 86: "those idiots from Pale . . .": Slobodan Milosevic, quoted in Holbrooke, *To End a War*, 256.

p. 89: "Let him go . . .": "General Guilty of Bosnia Genocide," *BBC News*, August 2, 2001, http://news.bbc.co.uk/2/hi/europe/1470928.stm (accessed January 23, 2009).

Chapter 5

p. 92: "The *janjaweed* killed . . .": Jonathan Harr, "Lives of the Saints," the *New Yorker*, January 5, 2009.

p. 93: "The *janjaweed* were making raids . . .": Harr, "Lives of the Saints," January 5, 2009.

p. 94: "intentionally directing attacks against . . .": International Criminal Court, quoted in "Warrant Issued for Sudan's Leader," *BBC News*, March 4, 2009, http://news.bbc.co.uk/2/hi/7923102. stm, (accessed March 4, 2009).

p. 94: "not be worth the ink . . .": Omar al-Bashir, quoted in "Warrant Issued for Sudan's Leader," March 4, 2009.

p. 94: "The biggest immediate threat . . .": Nicholas D. Kristof, "Watching Darfuris Die," the *New York Times*, March 7, 2009.

p. 96: "Thirty thousand Kurds . . .": Orhan Pamuk, quoted in *Das Magazin*, February 5, 2005.

p. 97: "today, after all, speaks of the annihilation . . .": Adolf Hitler, quoted in Peter Balakian, *The Burning Tigris*, New York: HarperCollins, 2003, 377.

p. 98: "The Federal government and the great majority . . .": Konrad Adenauer, speech to the Bundestag, Bonn, Germany, September 27, 1951.

p. 100: "We finally close the circle . . .": Ronald Reagan, quoted in Samantha Power, *"A Problem from Hell:" America and the Age of Genocide*, New York: HarperCollins Perennial, 2003, 18.

p. 102: "We, the international community . . .": Madeleine Albright, quoted in Philip Gourevitch, *We Wish to Inform You That Tomorrow We Will Be Killed With Our Families: Stories from Rwanda*, New York: Farrar, Straus, 1998, 350.

Further Information

Books

Altman, Linda Jacobs. *Genocide: The Systematic Killing of a People.* New Jersey: Enslow Publishers, 2009.

Etcheson, Craig. *After the Killing Fields: Lessons from the Cambodian Genocide.* Santa Barbara, CA: Praeger Publishers, 2005.

Fisanick, Christina. *Genocide.* Farmington Hills, MI: Greenhaven Press, 2007.

____. *Rwanda Genocide.* Farmington Hills, MI: Greenhaven Press, 2004.

Frey, Rebecca Joyce. *Genocide and International Justice.* New York: Facts on File, 2009.

January, Brendan. *Genocide: Modern Crimes Against Humanity.* Minneapolis: First Century Books/Lerner Publishing Group, 2007.

Perl, Lila, and Marion Blumenthal Lazan. *Four Perfect Pebbles: A Holocaust Story.* New York: Greenwillow/HarperCollins, 1996.

Pran, Dith, comp., and Kim, DePaul, ed., *Children of Cambodia's Killing Fields: Memoirs by Survivors.* New Haven: Yale University Press, 1997.

Xavier, John. *Darfur: African Genocide.* New York: Rosen, 2008.

Websites

Amnesty International (AI) is a nongovernmental organization (NGO) that operates worldwide to end human rights violations, including genocide, torture, and the death penalty. Founded in London, England, in 1961, it also advocates for the rights of women and children. AI won the Nobel Peace Prize in 1977.
www.amnesty.org

Doctors Without Borders/Médecins Sans Frontiéres (MSF) is an independent international organization created by doctors in France in 1971. It acts impartially in armed conflicts and in humanitarian crises of every kind to bring medical care to the needy, regardless of race, religion, or political affiliation. MSF received the Nobel Peace Prize in 1999.
www.doctorswithoutborders.org

European Court of Human Rights/Cour européenne des droits de l'homme (ECtHR) was established in Strasbourg, France, in 1950 by the forty-seven members of the Council of Europe to deal with violations of human rights by member states. The ECtHR has dealt with abuses by the Soviet Union and by post-Soviet Russia, by the United Kingdom in its treatment of Irish prisoners, and with other infractions committed by its European members.
http://echr.coe.int

Human Rights Watch (HRW) is a leading NGO that operates worldwide, researching and promoting human rights. It was founded in 1978 as Helsinki Watch (to monitor the treatment of political prisoners and other dissidents in the Soviet Union and its satellites). The organization was renamed and broadened in 1988 to work to prevent genocide, torture, capital punishment, child labor, and child soldiers, as well as to promote the legalization of abortion, gay rights, and the rights of AIDS patients.
www.hrw.org

International Committee of the Red Cross (ICRC) is the oldest private humanitarian organization, having been founded in 1863. War wounded, refugees, prisoners, and civilian disaster victims anywhere in the world are among its chief concerns. Its headquarters are in Geneva, Switzerland. The ICRC won Nobel Peace Prizes in 1917, 1944, and 1963.

www.icrc.org

International Criminal Court (ICC) is a permanent tribunal for the prosecution of individuals accused of genocide, war crimes, and crimes against humanity. It was established in 2002 following a statute adopted in Rome, Italy, in 1998, and is supported by more than one hundred member states. The ICC meets in The Hague, Netherlands. The United States, China, Russia, and India are not members of the ICC.

www.icc-cpi.int

United Nations High Commissioner for Refugees (UNHCR), established in 1950, was previously known as the United Nations Relief and Rehabilitation Administration (UNRRA). Headquartered in Geneva, Switzerland, UNHCR protects and supports refugee victims of war, genocide, natural disasters, and other catastrophic events throughout the world. UNHCR received Nobel Peace Prizes in 1954 and 1981.

www.unhcr.org

Bibliography

Akçam, Taner. *A Shameful Act: The Armenian Genocide and the Question of Turkish Responsibility*. New York: Metropolitan, Henry Holt, 2006.

Balakian, Peter. *The Burning Tigris: The Armenian Genocide and America's Response*. New York: HarperCollins, 2003.

Burr, J. Millard, and Robert O. Collins. *Darfur: The Long Road to Disaster*. Princeton, New Jersey: Markus Wiener, 2006.

Gilbert, Martin. *Auschwitz and the Allies*. New York: Holt, Rinehart and Winston, 1981.

Gourevitch, Philip. *We Wish to Inform You That Tomorrow We Will Be Killed With Our Families: Stories from Rwanda*. New York: Farrar, Straus, 1998.

Holbrooke, Richard. *To End a War*. New York: Random House, 1998.

Morgenthau, Henry Sr. *Ambassador Morgenthau's Story*. New York: Doubleday and Doran, 1918.

Power, Samantha. *"A Problem from Hell": America and the Age of Genocide.* New York: HarperCollins Perennial, 2003.

Prunier, Gérard. *Darfur: The Ambiguous Genocide.* Ithaca, New York: Cornell University Press, revised and updated edition, 2007.

_____. *The Rwanda Crisis: History of a Genocide.* New York: Columbia University Press, 1995.

Rieff, David. *Slaughterhouse: Bosnia and the Failure of the West.* New York: Simon & Schuster, 1995.

Short, Philip. *Pol Pot: Anatomy of a Nightmare.* New York: Henry Holt, 2004.

Silber, Laura, and Allan Little. *Yugoslavia: Death of a Nation.* New York: Penguin, 1996.

Steidle, Brian, and Gretchen Steidle Wallace. *The Devil Came on Horseback: Bearing Witness to the Genocide in Darfur.* New York: Public Affairs, Perseus, 2007.

Index

Page numbers in **boldface** are
illustrations, tables, and charts.

About the Author

LILA PERL has published more than sixty books for young people and adults, including fiction and nonfiction. Her nonfiction writings have been mainly in the fields of social history, family memoir, and biography. She has traveled extensively to do cultural and background studies of seven African countries, as well as China, Puerto Rico, Guatemala, and Mexico. She has written on subjects as diverse as foods and food customs, genealogy, Egyptian mummies, Latino popular culture, and the Holocaust.

Two of her books have been honored with American Library Association Notable awards: *Red-Flannel Hash and Shoo-Fly Pie* and *Four Perfect Pebbles*. Ten titles have been selected as Notable Children's Trade Books in the Field of Social Studies. Lila Perl has also received a Boston Globe Horn Book award, a Sidney Taylor Committee award, and a Young Adults' Choice award from the International Reading Association. The New York Public Library has cited her work among Best Books for the Teen Age. Her most recent book for Marshall Cavendish Benchmark was *Immigration*, in this series.

Lila Perl lives in Beechhurst, New York.

2/15 (2) 4/14